BASEBALL CHRONOLOGY

David Nemec

Publications International, Ltd.

David Nemec is a baseball historian who has authored or coauthored numerous baseball history, quiz, and memorabilia books, including *Great Baseball Feats, Facts & Firsts*; *The Ultimate Baseball Book*; and *20th Century Baseball Chronicle*. He has consulted on such books as *Greatest Baseball Players of All Time*, *Baseball: More Than 150 Years*, and *The Best of Baseball*.

Editorial Assistance: Marty Strasen

Front cover: **Brian Spurlock/SportsChrome USA**

Allsport USA: 343; Jonathan Daniel: 372; Tomasso Derosa: 364; Stephen Dunn: 368; Otto Greule, Jr.: 333; Doug Pensinger: 356; **AP/Wide World Photos:** 9, 292; Rusty Kennedy: 329; Hans Deryk: 349; Rick Bowmer: 353; **Chicago Historical Society:** 66; **National Baseball Library & Archive, Cooperstown, NY:** 11, 14, 29, 42, 44, 57, 59, 69, 89, 98, 101, 120, 123, 128, 140, 145, 148, 156, 159, 165, 170, 183, 188, 197, 205, 213, 215, 271, 277; **Transcendental Graphics:** 104, 296.

All rights reserved under International and Pan American copyright conventions. Copyright © 2000 Publications International, Ltd. This publication may not be reproduced or quoted in whole or in part by any means whatsoever without written permission from Louis Weber, CEO of Publications International, Ltd., 7373 North Cicero Avenue, Lincolnwood, Illinois 60712. Permission is never granted for commercial purposes. Printed in U.S.A.

Contents

Introduction	8
1901: American League is born	10
1902: AL loses Milwaukee, McGraw	13
1903: Boston wins first-ever World Series	16
1904: McGraw's Giants refuse to play in Series	19
1905: Mathewson lifts Giants in "Shutout Series"	22
1906: Brown leads Cubs to 116 wins	25
1907: Cubs call themselves champions	28
1908: Merkle's miscue costs Giants the pennant	31
1909: Cobb wins lone Triple Crown	34
1910: Mack steers A's to Series triumph	37
1911: Baker's Series blasts earn him a nickname	40
1912: Snodgrass gaffe costs Giants against Boston	43
1913: A's cop third Series in four years	46
1914: Federal League becomes a third major league	49
1915: Phillies make meteoric rise to pennant	52
1916: Giants win 26 in a row	55
1917: White Sox go all the way	58
1918: War effort shortens season, claims life of Grant	61
1919: Scandalous Sox hand Series to Reds	64
1920: Boston sells its Babe	67
1921: Giants outlast Yankees in "Subway Series"	70

1922: *Giants frustrate Yanks again*	73
1923: *Ruth bats .393, takes home first MVP trophy*	76
1924: *Washington prevails in Series thriller*	79
1925: *Hornsby cops second Triple Crown*	82
1926: *Phils overcome Babe's Series blasts*	85
1927: *"Murderer's Row" terrorizes opposing pitchers*	88
1928: *Gehrig, Ruth help Yanks dominate Series*	91
1929: *A's ride 10-run inning to Series victory*	94
1930: *Wilson amasses 190 RBI*	97
1931: *Cards go seven to beat A's*	100
1932: *Ruth's Series shot: Called?*	103
1933: *Foxx, Klein win Triple Crowns*	106
1934: *Dean machine turns tide in Series*	109
1935: *Cubs win 21 straight, lose to Tigers in Series*	112
1936: *Cobb leads first inductees into Hall*	115
1937: *Medwick wears the Triple Crown*	118
1938: *Vander Meer fires back-to-back no-hitters*	122
1939: *Gehrig delivers emotional farewell speech*	126
1940: *Reds maintain MVP streak, win Series*	130
1941: *DiMaggio hits in 56 straight games*	134
1942: *Triple Crown, not MVP, goes to Williams*	138
1943: *Yankees find way back to summit*	142
1944: *Browns end their record slump with only pennant*	146
1945: *Tigers foil Cubs in seven-game Series*	150
1946: *Brecheen picks up three Series wins*	154

1947: *Robinson breaks color barrier*	158
1948: *Boudreau gains glory as player, skipper*	162
1949: *Stengel debuts with world title*	166
1950: *Sisler's homer lifts Phils on final day*	170
1951: *Thomson launches shot heard 'round the world*	174
1952: *Yanks win Series on the road*	178
1953: *Make it a high five for the Yanks*	182
1954: *Giants pull off Series stunner*	186
1955: *Dodgers end long string of Series misery*	190
1956: *Larsen picture perfect in Series milestone*	194
1957: *Giants, Dodgers to switch coasts*	198
1958: *Yanks storm back to win Series*	202
1959: *Mr. Cub repeats as NL MVP*	206
1960: *Maz's memorable blast powers Pirates*	210
1961: *Maris eclipses Ruth's long-ball record*	214
1962: *Terry, Yanks blank Giants in Game 7*	218
1963: *Koufax, Dodgers blow away Yanks*	222
1964: *Cards hand Yanks second straight Series loss*	226
1965: *Koufax, Dodgers reign supreme*	230
1966: *Robinson takes Triple Crown*	234
1967: *Red Sox soar to first before Series setback*	238
1968: *Tigers pull off unlikely Series comeback*	242
1969: *"Miracle Mets" enjoy ride of a lifetime*	246
1970: *Orioles ride home run barrage to title*	250
1971: *A's leave hitters feeling Blue*	254
1972: *Tenace nets A's a Series crown*	258

1973: *Break-even Mets push A's to limit*	262
1974: *Aaron breaks Ruth's hallowed HR mark*	266
1975: *Reds prevail in Series classic*	270
1976: *Big Red Machine defends crown*	274
1977: *"Mr. October" powers the Yankees*	278
1978: *Yanks again leave Dodgers blue*	282
1979: *"Pops" has Pirates dancing*	286
1980: *Phillies end championship drought*	290
1981: *Baseball strikes out, Reds lose out*	294
1982: *Henderson swipes stolen base record*	298
1983: *Orioles treat Altobelli to world title*	302
1984: *Tigers start 35-5, roar to title*	306
1985: *Rose becomes the all-time hit king*	310
1986: *Mets stage Series rally*	314
1987: *Surprising Twins roll past Cards in Series*	318
1988: *Hobbled Gibson homers in a pinch*	322
1989: *Quake shakes Bay Area, Series*	326
1990: *Reds cut off A's power*	330
1991: *Twins, Braves rise from worst to first*	334
1992: *Series trophy moves north of border*	338
1993: *Carter blasts Jays to second straight title*	342
1994: *Strike wipes out World Series*	346
1995: *Ripken breaks Gehrig's record*	350
1996: *Wetteland saves day for champion Yanks*	354
1997: *Marlins land the big one in just five years*	358
1998: *Big Mac outslugs Sosa, Maris*	362
1999: *Yanks win 25th world title*	366
Index	370

Introduction

On April 17, 1953, Yankee Mickey Mantle blasted a ball 565 feet—one of the longest home runs ever recorded. Later in the game, he bunted for a hit.

Welcome to *Baseball Chronology*, the most baseball a fan could possibly hold in one hand. Not only is it a terrific historical book, but it's loaded with fascinating facts.

This unique reference tool recounts baseball's most significant events since 1901, the first year of the American League and the birth of the modern major leagues. For each season you'll find:

- Statistical leaders—batting champs, home run kings, strikeout leaders, and so on.
- Award winners, such as Most Valuable Players and Cy Young honorees.
- Pennant-race stories and postseason synopses.
- Amazing single-game feats, such as David Cone's perfect game and Mike Schmidt's four-homer afternoon.
- Career milestones, such as Hank Aaron's 715th home run and Nolan Ryan's 300th win.
- Events that impacted on the game, such as the Black Sox scandal and the earthquake that shook the 1989 World Series.
- Extraordinary feats in the Negro Leagues and minor leagues.
- Blockbuster trades, outrageous contracts, and the opening of new ballparks.

Baseball Chronology is also peppered with fascinating facts, trivia, and anecdotes. During the war years, you'll learn about Joe Nuxhall, a 15-year-old Reds hurler; Pete Gray, the Browns' one-armed outfielder; and Bert Shepard, Washington's one-legged pitcher. In 1978, Graig Nettles described life under George Steinbrenner: "When I was a little boy, I wanted to be a baseball player and join the circus. With the Yankees, I've accomplished both."

Inform and delight yourself with the nuggets of *Baseball Chronology*, the peanuts and crackerjack of baseball history.

Willie Mays and Mickey Mantle

1901

American League is born... Lajoie wins Triple Crown... Pittsburgh, Chicago claim the first modern-day pennants

- The first AL game is played on April 24—Chicago 8, Cleveland 2.

- St. Louis's Jesse Burkett leads the NL in batting (.382), runs (139), and hits (228).

- Philly's Nap Lajoie leads the AL in BA (.422), homers (14), RBI (125), hits (229), doubles (48), total bases (345), runs (145), SA (.635), and OBP (.451).

- Boston's Cy Young leads both major leagues with 33 wins and a 1.62 ERA.

- Connie Mack manages the fledgling Philadelphia A's and will be their only manager until 1951.

- Pirate Honus Wagner leads the NL in steals (49) and RBI (126) while batting .353.

- The modern infield-fly rule is adopted.

- For the first time in the NL, foul balls are counted as strikes one and two. All fouls in the AL are strikes, no matter the count.

- Cleveland's Earl Moore earns a somewhat dubious distinction on May 9, no-hitting the White Sox for nine innings but losing 4-2 in ten.

> **"If you pitched inside to him, he'd tear the hand off the third baseman, and if you pitched him outside he'd knock down the second baseman."**
>
> —*Ed Walsh on Nap Lajoie*

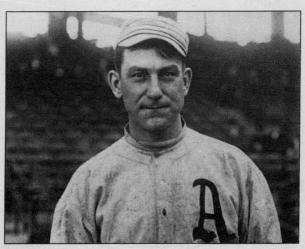

Nap Lajoie

- Cincinnati's Noodles Hahn strikes out an NL-best 239 batters on his way to 22 victories, a modern record for pitching wins for a last-place team. Sixteen of his strikeouts, a post-1893 record, come in a May 22 game against Boston.

- Baltimore's Willie Keeler collects at least 200 hits for the eighth consecutive year, a major-league record.

- The A's and Senators complete a marathon stretch, playing five consecutive doubleheaders against each other in August.

- Philadelphia's Chick Fraser hits an AL-record 31 batters.

- Pittsburgh claims its first NL pennant, beating out the Phillies, with a pair of 20-game winners in Deacon Phillippe and Jack Chesbro.

- Chicago wins the inaugural AL flag.

> On May 23, Nap Lajoie becomes the first player in baseball history to be intentionally walked with the bases loaded.

1902

AL loses Milwaukee, McGraw... Chesbro hurls 41 straight shutout innings... Minor-leaguer slugs eight homers in one game

- Milwaukee moves to St. Louis—the AL's first franchise shift.

- Pittsburgh's Honus Wagner leads the NL in runs (105), RBI (91), doubles (33), SA (.467), and steals (42).

- Pittsburgh's Jack Chesbro leads the NL in wins (28) and winning pct. (.824) and pitches 41 consecutive scoreless innings.

- John McGraw jumps from the AL in midseason to manage the Giants.

- Washington's Ed Delahanty wins the AL batting title (.378). He won the NL title in 1899.

- The *Chicago Daily News* coins the nickname "Cubs" for the city's NL team. It had been called "Colts" and "Orphans."

Cy Young

- Pirate Ginger Beaumont leads the NL in batting (.357) and hits (194).

- Boston's Cy Young leads the AL in wins (32) and complete games (41).

- Harry Pulliam is named NL president.

- Nig Clarke of Corsicana (Texas League) hits eight homers in as many at-bats.

- Detroit's Ed Siever becomes the first sub-.500 pitcher to lead his league in ERA (1.91).

- Pittsburgh's Tommy Leach leads the NL with six homers, fewest by a league leader in the 20th century.

- The legendary Cubs infield trio of Joe Tinker, Johnny Evers, and Frank Chance takes the field together for the first time in a September game.

- Cardinals Jack and Mike O'Neill form the first brother battery in NL history.

> **"Today they seem to think that the most exciting play in baseball is the home run. But in my book, the most exciting play in baseball is a three-bagger, or an inside-the-park home run."**
>
> —*Pittsburgh's Tommy Leach*

- Sam Mertes of the White Sox plays all nine positions during the season.

- The Pirates repeat their NL pennant, running away from Brooklyn by 27½ games.

- The Philadelphia A's win their first AL flag.

1903

Delahanty tumbles to his death... Baseball debuts in moving pictures... Boston wins first-ever World Series

- The AL's Baltimore team moves to New York, the last franchise move until 1953.

- Foul balls are counted as strikes by both leagues for the first time.

- Cleveland's Nap Lajoie leads the AL in batting average (.355) and slugging percentage (.533).

- Pirate Ginger Beaumont leads the NL in hits (209), runs (137), and total bases (272).

- Washington star Ed Delahanty falls from a railway trestle over Niagara Falls to his death. Some say he had been ordered off a train at Fort Erie by the conductor and was chasing it on foot as it crossed a bridge.

- Boston's Buck Freeman leads the AL in homers (13), total bases (281), and RBI (104).

- When part of the Phillies' park—the Baker Bowl—collapses, 12 fans are killed.

- Giant Christy Mathewson tops the NL in strikeouts (267) and wins 30 games. Teammate Joe McGinnity pitches 434 innings and wins 31 games.

- Athletics pitcher Rube Waddell strikes out 302 batters, a post-1893 record.

- Baseball's first moving picture is made, featuring Lajoie and Cleveland teammate Harry Bay.

The 1903 World Series winner's share, given to each member of the Boston Pilgrims, is $1,182.

- The Pirates hold their opposition scoreless over a record 57 consecutive innings.

- Gambler Frank Ferrell and Bill Devery, reputedly a crooked cop, become owners of New York's AL team.

- Jack Doscher becomes the first son of an ex-major-leaguer to play in the majors.

- Bill Keister hits .320 and leads the Phillies in home runs and RBI, but the team cuts him after the season.

> **"You can learn little from victory. You can learn everything from defeat."**
> —*Christy Mathewson of the Giants*

- The Pirates win their third consecutive NL pennant. Boston wins the AL flag.

- Pittsburgh and Boston meet in the first modern World Series, with the first game taking place at the Pilgrims' Huntington Grounds. Boston falls behind three games to one but takes the next four in a row for a 5-3 victory over the favored Pirates.

- Pilgrims pitcher Deacon Phillippe posts a 3-2 record in the Series, with five complete games and a 2.86 ERA.

Young pitches perfect game... Boston cops AL flag on final day... McGraw's Giants refuse to play in Series

- Both leagues expand their schedules to 154 games.

- Highlander Jack Chesbro's 41 wins and 48 complete games set post-1900 ML records.

- Rube Waddell of the A's fans 349, setting an all-time ML record for a 154-game season.

> Joe McGinnity and Christy Mathewson set a modern record for wins by teammates with 35 and 33, respectively, during the Giants' pennant-winning season.

- Pittsburgh's Honus Wagner leads the NL in BA (.349), SA (.520), total bases (255), doubles (44), and steals (53).

- Cleveland's Nap Lajoie leads the AL in BA (.381), SA (.554), hits (211), total bases (307), RBI (102), and doubles (50).

- Giant Joe McGinnity leads the NL in wins (35), winning pct. (.814), ERA (1.61), shutouts (nine), innings (408), and saves (five).

> **The Cardinals' Jack Taylor and Boston's Vic Willis share a season record by pitching 39 consecutive complete games.**

- Cy Young of the Pilgrims pitches the first perfect game of the 20th century on May 5. He also becomes the first to pitch no-hitters in two different centuries.

- Cleveland is the only AL team to average four runs per game, marking the start of what becomes known as the dead-ball era.

- Giant Christy Mathewson wins 33 and leads the NL in Ks (212).

- Washington sets a 20th-century record for losses in a season with 113.

- The Phillies' John Lush, at 18, becomes the youngest regular NL player in history.

- Harry Davis of the A's leads the AL in homers (with 10) for the first of four straight years.

- Frank Huelsman plays for a record four different AL teams in the same season.

- Bill Dinneen is the Pilgrims' marathon man, pitching 337 innings without being relieved. He posts a 23-14 ledger.

- Boston wins the AL championship on the last day of the season. The Pilgrims enter a season-ending doubleheader against New York a game and a half ahead of the Highlanders, then win the opener 3-2.

- The Giants win the NL pennant, giving John McGraw his first flag as a manager. They refuse to play Boston in the World Series, though, calling the AL a "minor league." NL President Harry Pulliam supports the decision.

1905

Chicago teams baffle opposing hitters... Name change honors Lajoie... Mathewson lifts Giants in "Shutout Series"

- Cincinnati's Cy Seymour leads the NL in BA (.377), SA (.559), RBI (121), hits (219), doubles (40), triples (21), and total bases (325). He misses a Triple Crown by one home run.

- Cleveland's Elmer Flick leads the AL in BA (.306), SA (.466), and triples (19).

- Philly's Rube Waddell leads the AL in wins (26), ERA (1.48), and Ks (287).

- Giant Christy Mathewson leads the NL in wins (31), ERA (1.27), Ks (206), winning pct. (.795), and shutouts (eight).

- Philly's Harry Davis tops the AL in homers (eight), RBI (83), doubles (47), and runs (92).

- Waddell beats Boston's Cy Young in a 20-inning game on July 4.

Christy Mathewson

- Vic Willis of Boston (NL) loses a modern ML-record 29 games.

- Boston (NL) sets a record with four 20-game losers.

- The dead-ball era goes on. The A's lead the AL with 623 runs, fewest ever by a loop leader.

- The White Sox register a team ERA of 1.99, while the Cubs are not far behind at 2.04. Both set records for their respective leagues.

- Nap Lajoie becomes Cleveland's player/manager, and the team becomes known as the "Naps" in his honor.

- Giants manager John McGraw is suspended for 15 games and fined $150 by the NL for abusing umpires.

- Connie Mack guides the A's to their first AL pennant by two games. Waddell, Eddie Plank, and Andy Coakley combine for 71 victories.

> Cleveland catcher Nig Clarke secretly wears soccer shin guards under his uniform during the 1905 season, the first step toward formal shin protectors for backstops.

- The Giants beat Pittsburgh by nine games for their second straight NL flag, and McGraw agrees to play in the World Series after refusing the year before.

- New York wins the Series, four games to one, with every game a shutout. Mathewson hurls three of them for the victorious Giants.

Crosstown Series goes to White Sox... Brown leads Cubs to 116 wins... Taylor's string of complete games halted

- The White Sox win 19 straight games, an all-time AL record, en route to the pennant.

- St. Louis's George Stone leads the AL in BA (.358), SA (.501), and total bases (291).

- Pittsburgh's Honus Wagner tops the NL in BA (.339), doubles (38), and total bases (237).

- The Boston Beaneaters' Johnny Bates becomes the first player in the 20th century to hit a home run in his first at-bat in the majors.

- The Cubs set modern ML records for wins (116) and fewest runs allowed (381) in winning the NL flag with a .763 winning pct.

- The Cubs' Three Finger Brown leads the NL with a 1.04 ERA and 10 shutouts. It's the lowest ERA ever for a pitcher with at least 250 innings.

- Cardinal Jack Taylor's streak of 118 consecutive complete games ends.

- On September 1, Joe Harris of Boston and Jack Coombs of the A's duel 24 innings. The A's win 4-1.

- Doc White of the White Sox leads the league with a 1.52 ERA, walking only 38 in 219 innings.

- New York's Al Orth leads the AL in wins (27) and complete games (36).

> **"It was a hard Series to lose, but you can't win all the time."**
>
> —*Frank Chance, Cubs infielder*

- While out with an injury, Jake Beckley of St. Louis is hired by the NL as an umpire.

- Detroit's Herman Schaefer slides into every base after clubbing a pinch-hit home run in Chicago. In another game, against Cleveland, he "steals" first base from second in order to give teammate Davy Jones a chance to score from third base on a subsequent double steal.

- Giants manager John McGraw gets into another fight, this time with rookie infielder Paul Sentell of the Phillies.

The Cubs post a 60-15 record away from home.

- Brooklyn's Harry McIntire takes a no-hitter into the 11th inning against the Pirates, but he winds up losing 1-0.

- Center fielder Chick Stahl is named manager of Boston's AL club after Jimmy Collins is fired.

- Christy Mathewson's brother, Henry, walks 14 batters in his only start in the majors.

- The White Sox, dubbed the "Hitless Wonders" while batting .230 during the regular season, score eight runs in each of the last two World Series games to beat the crosstown Cubs, four games to two. It marks the first time two teams from the same city meet in a World Series.

1907

Boston pulls for its Sox...Doubleday credited with game's invention...Cubs call themselves champions

- Detroit's Ty Cobb leads the AL in BA (.350), hits (212), SA (.473), RBI (116), total bases (286), and steals (49).

- Pittsburgh's Honus Wagner easily tops the NL in BA (.350), SA (.513), total bases (264), doubles (38), and steals (61).

- Pilgrims player/manager Chick Stahl, 34, commits suicide during the preseason by drinking carbolic acid in an Indiana hotel room.

- The Giants' Christy Mathewson leads the NL in wins (24) and Ks (178).

- Jack Pfiester tops the NL in ERA (1.15), as the Cubs have four of the loop's top five in ERA.

- Chicago's Ed Walsh hurls 422 innings and leads the AL in complete games (37) and ERA (1.60).

Honus Wagner

- Philly's Rube Waddell wins his seventh, and last, AL K crown (232).

- Philly's Harry Davis wins his fourth straight AL homer crown (eight).

- The 40-year-old Cy Young enjoys another dominant season, winning 22 games with a 1.99 ERA.

- Washington steals an AL-record 13 bases against New York and catcher Branch Rickey.

- For the first time, Boston's AL team is called the Red Sox.

- Walter Johnson makes his debut in the majors. The Washington pitcher loses his opener to the Tigers 3-2 but comes back with a 7-2, four-hit victory over Cleveland.

- Al Spalding creates a commission to unearth the origins of baseball. Based largely on the vague testimony of one witness to what was purported to have been the first game, Abner Doubleday is credited with the game's invention.

- The Tigers claim their first AL championship, with a 20-year-old Cobb leading the way.

- The Cubs repeat their NL pennant by a whopping 17 games over Pittsburgh.

- Chicago whips Detroit in the World Series, winning four straight games after a 3-3 tie in the opener.

With 20 of the Tigers' 58 losses, George Mullin becomes the first pitcher to lose 20 games for a pennant winner.

1908

Baseball sings an anthem...Merkle's miscue costs Giants the pennant...Cubs repeat as Series champs

- White Sox hurler Ed Walsh leads the AL in wins (40), winning pct. (.727), Ks (269), complete games (42), shutouts (11), and innings (464—a 20th-century record).

- Detroit's Ty Cobb wins the AL bat crown (.324) and also leads in SA (.475), total bases (276), RBI (108), hits (188), doubles (36), and triples (20).

- Pirate Honus Wagner tops the NL in BA (.354), hits (201), steals (53), RBI (109), doubles (39), triples (19), SA (.542), and total bases (308).

- Giant Christy Mathewson leads the NL in wins (37), ERA (1.43), Ks (259), shutouts (12), complete games (34), innings (391), and saves (five). It marks the last time he will win 30 or more games.

- Washington's Walter Johnson pitches three shutouts in four days vs. New York.

- Cleveland's Addie Joss pitches a perfect game over Chicago on October 2. Joss leads the AL in ERA (1.16).

- Sam Crawford of the Tigers leads the AL with seven homers, becoming the first player to ever win home run titles in both leagues.

New York's Highlanders slump to a 51-103 record, but interim manager Kid Elberfeld goes 27-21.

- The Cubs win the NL pennant by one game when Fred Merkle of the Giants makes his famous blunder, failing to touch second base on Al Bridwell's apparent game-winning single at the Polo Grounds. The Cubs, who retire Merkle on the controversial force out, will later win a make-up game to claim the flag.

- The Cubs' Ed Reulbach pitches two shutouts on the same day, blanking Brooklyn by scores of 5-0 and 3-0. He yields a total of eight hits while striking out 10.

- The song "Take Me Out to the Ballgame" is first introduced to the public. It will eventually become baseball's unofficial anthem.

> **"If this game goes to Chicago by any trick or argument, you can take it from me that if we lose the pennant thereby, I will never play professional baseball again."**
>
> —Christy Mathewson, before the Giants' make-up game with the Cubs is slated for New York

- The Chicago DP combo of Tinker to Evers to Chance is immortalized in a poem.

- Detroit records triple plays against the Red Sox in back-to-back games.

- Detroit repeats its AL title by a half-game.

- The Cubs beat Detroit in the World Series by a 4-1 margin. It will be the Cubs' last Series championship of the century.

- Chicago's Three Finger Brown notches a Series ERA of 0.00 in 11 innings.

1909

Young returns to Lake Erie's shore... Cobb wins his lone Triple Crown... Forbes, Shibe open their gates

- Cy Young is traded from the Red Sox to Cleveland, where he started his major-league career in 1890. He winds up winning 19 games. In return, the Red Sox get pitchers Charlie Chech and Jack Ryan, plus $12,500.

- Pittsburgh's Honus Wagner leads the NL in BA (.339), SA (.489), total bases (242), doubles (39), and RBI (100).

- Detroit's Ty Cobb wins his only AL Triple Crown (.377, nine, 107). Cobb also leads in SA (.517), total bases (296), hits (216), runs (116), and steals (76).

- Detroit's George Mullin leads the AL in wins (29) and winning pct. (.784).

- Forbes Field and Shibe Park open—the first all-concrete-and-steel stadiums.

- Philly's Harry Krause leads the AL in ERA (1.39).

- On July 19, Cleveland shortstop Neal Ball performs the majors' first unassisted triple play.

- Chicago's Three Finger Brown leads the NL in wins (27), complete games (32), and saves (seven).

- Giant Christy Mathewson goes 25-6 and posts an ML-leading 1.14 ERA.

- The Giants' Leon Ames no-hits Brooklyn for nine innings on Opening Day, but he winds up losing 3-0 in 13 frames, with seven hits against him.

"Baseball is in its infancy."

—*Brooklyn owner Charlie Ebbets*

- Cleveland's Tris Speaker leads AL outfielders in putouts, assists, and double plays.

- The Phillies get rained out for a record 10 consecutive games.

- NL President Harry Pulliam shoots himself in the head in a room at the New York Athletic Club. He dies the following day.

- The Cubs win 104 games but lose the NL pennant to the Pirates and their 110-42 record. Pittsburgh holds first place from May 5 through the end of the season.

- The AL crown goes to the Tigers for the third year in a row, although Connie Mack's rising A's made an interesting race of it.

- The Pirates win the most exciting World Series to date, four games to three. Pittsburgh rookie right-hander Babe Adams wins three complete games, including the deciding contest by an 8-0 score.

> John Kull of the A's wins his only pitching appearance, handles his only fielding chance cleanly, and gets a hit in his only big-league at-bat, making him the only man in history with a 1.000 mark in all three categories.

1910

AL batting title muddied by controversy... Comiskey Park begins long run... Mack steers A's to Series triumph

- Phillie Sherry Magee tops the NL in BA (.331), SA (.507), RBI (123), runs (110), and total bases (263).

- Philly's Jack Coombs leads the AL with 31 wins and 13 shutouts (an all-time AL record).

- William Taft is the first president to throw out the first ball.

- Comiskey Park, home of the White Sox, opens for play.

- Washington's Walter Johnson leads the AL in Ks (313), complete games (38), and innings (373).

- Cleveland's Nap Lajoie leads the AL in hits (227), doubles (51), and total bases (304).

- Cleveland's Cy Young wins No. 500 on July 19.

- Detroit's Sam Crawford tops the AL in triples (19), RBI (120), and runs produced (198).

- The Cubs' King Cole leads the NL and sets a rookie record for winning percentage (.833) by going 20-4. His ERA of 1.80 is the lowest in the league.

- Christy Mathewson of the Giants leads the NL in wins (27) for the final time.

- Lajoie edges Ty Cobb for the batting title under questionable circumstances. While Cobb sits out the last game with a .383 average, Lajoie has eight hits in a season-ending doubleheader against St. Louis to win with a .384 mark. Seven of those eight hits are bunt singles, with Browns third baseman John Corriden playing deep under manager Jack O'Connor's orders.

Earl Mack becomes the first big-leaguer in history to be managed by his father when he suits up for the A's under Connie Mack.

- In an effort to produce more scoring, both leagues introduce a new "jackrabbit" ball during the season.

- Two amateur teams play the first night game at Comiskey Park.

> **"We figured he did not have the nerve to bunt every time."**
>
> *—Browns manager Jack O'Connor after Nap Lajoie's eight-hit doubleheader to end the season*

- The Cubs' Joe Tinker becomes the first player to steal home twice in the same game.

- Frank Chance's Cubs take their fourth NL pennant in five years.

- Connie Mack's A's dominate the AL.

- The A's win the World Series in five games. Only a dramatic, come-from-behind Cubs victory in Game 4 keeps the Series from being a sweep.

- Eddie Collins and Frank Baker each hit over .400 for the A's in the Series.

Fire destroys Polo Grounds...Schulte, Cobb receive first MVP Awards...Baker's Series blasts earn him a nickname

- Cub Wildfire Schulte wins the first Chalmers Award (MVP) in the NL. Schulte tops the league in homers (21), SA (.534), RBI (121), and total bases (308).

- Ty Cobb receives the first AL Chalmers Award. Cobb leads the AL in BA (.420), RBI (144), steals (83), SA (.621), hits (248), runs (147), doubles (47), triples (24), and total bases (367). He also hits in 40 straight games, an AL record.

- Cleveland rookie Vean Gregg wins 23 games and tops the AL in ERA (1.81).

- Phillie Pete Alexander wins 28 games—a 20th-century ML rookie record. He also strikes out a rookie-record 227 batters.

- Cleveland's Joe Jackson hits .408 to set an ML rookie record.

- The Polo Grounds—the Giants' home—is ravaged by fire and has to be rebuilt. Another fire in the grandstand of the Senators' park closes that facility for weeks, and a third significant fire destroys the Mills Commission's evidence on the origins of baseball.

- Giant Christy Mathewson posts 26 wins and leads the NL in ERA at 1.99.

- Pittsburgh's Honus Wagner, with a .334 average, claims his final batting title by a single point.

- Cy Young beats Pittsburgh 1-0 for his final career win.

> **"If anybody was ever a better pitcher than that guy, I wouldn't know what his name was. It was just a pleasure to watch him work, even though he was beating your brains out most of the time."**
>
> —*Burleigh Grimes, describing Pete Alexander*

- Both leagues adopt the dual-umpire system for every game.

- Popular Cleveland pitcher Addie Joss, with a career record of 160-97, dies from meningitis. His 1.89 career ERA is the second lowest in history.

- The Giants win 20 of their last 24 games to beat Chicago by seven and a half for the NL pennant.

- Helen Britton becomes the first woman to own a major-league team when she takes control of the Cardinals.

- The A's repeat their AL flag, with 101 wins against 50 losses.

- The A's topple the Giants in six games in the World Series, scoring 13 runs in the final game.

- Philly's Frank Baker hits .375 with two home runs and five RBI in the Series, earning the nickname "Home Run."

Ty Cobb

1912

Marquard wins 19 straight... Shoeless Joe races to triples mark... Snodgrass gaffe costs Giants against Boston

- Three new parks open—Fenway Park, Navin Field (later to be named Tiger Stadium), and Redland Field (later Crosley Field).

- Giants second baseman Larry Doyle wins the NL Chalmers Award.

- Boston's Tris Speaker sets an AL record for doubles (53) and wins the Chalmers.

- Cub Heinie Zimmerman tops the NL in BA (.372), SA (.571), total bases (318), hits (207), RBI (103), homers (14), and doubles (41).

- Detroit's Ty Cobb leads the AL in BA (.410), SA (.586), and hits (227).

- Boston's Joe Wood tops the AL in wins (34), winning pct. (.872), shutouts (10), and complete games (35).

Joe Wood

> **"Can I throw harder than Joe Wood? Listen, my friend, there's no man alive who can throw harder than Joe Wood."**
>
> —*Washington's Walter Johnson*

- Cleveland's Joe Jackson hits .395 with 26 triples (an AL record).

- Washington's Walter Johnson wins 32 and tops the AL in Ks (303) and ERA (1.39).

- Giant Rube Marquard wins 19 straight games.

- Home Run Baker of the A's leads the AL with 130 RBI and ties for the home run title with 10.

- Twice in an 11-day period, Philly's Eddie Collins steals six bases in a game.

- Chief Wilson of the Pirates cracks an all-time record 36 triples.

- Boston's NL team is called the "Braves" for the first time.

- Homer and Tommy Thompson of New York (AL) become baseball's first brother battery.

- Cobb is suspended for going into the stands in New York and fighting with a heckler, who is missing one hand and part of another because of a workplace accident.

- The Giants successfully defend their NL flag.

- The Red Sox prevail in the AL.

- Boston wins the World Series in eight games (the second game is a 6-6, 11-inning tie, called because of darkness). The last game is a 3-2 decision in 10 innings, the key play coming when the Giants' Fred Snodgrass drops a fly ball for a two-base error in the ninth.

Mathewson offers no free rides ... Ebbets opens doors to Dodgers ... A's cop third Series in four years

- Ebbets Field in Brooklyn opens for play. Casey Stengel hits an inside-the-park home run in an exhibition game to help christen the park.

- The New York Highlanders first become called the New York Yankees.

- Brooklyn's Jake Daubert tops the NL in BA (.350) and wins the Chalmers Award.

- Washington's Walter Johnson takes the Chalmers Award in the AL. He tops the loop in wins (36), ERA (1.09), Ks (243), winning pct. (.837), complete games (29), and shutouts (11).

- Johnson hurls 55⅔ consecutive scoreless innings, a 20th-century AL record.

- Detroit's Ty Cobb again tops the AL in BA with a .390 mark.

- Philly's Gavvy Cravath tops the NL in hits (179), homers (19), total bases (298), SA (.568), and RBI (128).

- Tom Seaton of the Phils tops the NL with 27 wins and 168 Ks.

- White Sox Joe Jackson leads the AL in SA (.551), hits (197), and doubles (39).

- Philly's Home Run Baker leads the AL in homers (12) and RBI (126).

> **"Brooklyn has supported a losing team better than any other city on earth. Such a patronage deserves every convenience and comfort that can be provided at a baseball park, and that is what I hope to provide."**
>
> —*Brooklyn owner Charlie Ebbets*

- The Giants' Christy Mathewson throws an NL-record 68 consecutive innings without allowing a walk. His average for the season is 0.62 walks per game.

- Three members of the Athletics' "$100,000 infield" bat .326 or better.

- The "outlaw" Federal League locates teams in eight cities, including Chicago and Brooklyn, and vows to become a third major league by the following season.

- Honus Wagner and Nap Lajoie reach the .300 mark in hitting for the final time in their stellar careers.

- Frank Chance is hired to manage New York's AL team.

- Washington rookie Mel Acosta, age 17, becomes the youngest player to collect a pinch hit in AL history.

- The Giants post their second straight 100-win season, clinching the NL pennant well before the end of the summer.

- The A's win the AL flag over second-place Washington.

- The A's take the Series for the third time in four years. They need just five games to defeat the Giants. Baker bats .450 in the Series and drives home seven runs.

Federal League becomes a third major league... Ruth makes big-league debut... Braves shock champion A's in four-game sweep

- Baseball's National Commission recognizes the Fraternity of Professional Baseball Players of America and agrees to several conditions. Among them: teams will pay for uniforms, there will be no discrimination against Fraternity members, and outfield fences will be painted green to provide better background for batters.

- The last of the Cubs' Tinker-to-Evers-to-Chance double-play combination, Johnny Evers, is traded to the Braves for infielder Bill Sweeney and cash.

- Jake Ruppert and Til Houston purchase the New York team that's now universally known as the Yankees. Roger Peckinpaugh, age 23, becomes the youngest manager ever.

- The Federal League debuts as a third major league, with 172 former AL and NL players.

- Weeghman Field, now known as Wrigley Field, opens as home of the Federal League's Chicago Whales.

- The Braves' Johnny Evers wins the NL Chalmers Award.

- Philly's Eddie Collins (loop-high 122 runs) is the Chalmers winner in the AL.

- Washington's Walter Johnson leads the majors in wins (28), shutouts (nine), complete games (33), and Ks (225).

> **"Ruth made a grave mistake when he gave up pitching. Working once a week, he might have lasted a long time and become a great star."**
>
> —*Tris Speaker*

- Phillie Pete Alexander leads the NL in complete games (32), strikeouts (214), and wins (27).

- Honus Wagner and Nap Lajoie each collect their 3,000th hit.

- Red Sox Dutch Leonard posts a 20th-century record-low 1.01 ERA.

- Red Sox Babe Ruth makes his major-league debut on July 11. He strikes out the first batter he faces, Jack Graney, and allows eight hits in seven innings against Cleveland. He gets a no-decision.

- Phillie Sherry Magee leads the NL in hits (171), RBI (103), doubles (39), SA (.509), and total bases (277).

- Detroit's Ty Cobb leads the ML in BA (.368) and SA (.513).

- Chicago's Jim Scott no-hits Washington, but loses 1-0 in 10 innings.

- Rube Waddell dies at age 37.

- The "Miracle" Braves climb from last place on July 4 to first by the end of the season, winning their first NL pennant of the century. They win 34 of their last 44 games.

- The A's win their fourth AL flag in five seasons, but fail to repeat as World Series champs when the Braves sweep them in a huge upset. Hank Gowdy, a .243 hitter during the season, bats .545 with five extra-base hits for Boston.

1915

Federal League folds up tent... Phillies make meteoric rise to pennant... Red Sox win Series in five

- Detroit's Ty Cobb leads the AL in BA (.369), total bases (274), runs (144), hits (208), and steals (an ML-record 96).

- Washington's Walter Johnson tops the AL in wins (27), complete games (35), and Ks (203).

- Phillie Pete Alexander tops the NL in wins (31), ERA (1.22), complete games (36), strikeouts (241), and shutouts (12).

- The Phils' Gavvy Cravath hits an ML-record 24 homers. He leads the NL in RBI (115), SA (.510), total bases (266), runs (89), and walks (86).

- New York's Larry Doyle tops the NL in BA (.320), doubles (40), and hits (189).

- Eddie Plank becomes the first southpaw to win 300 games.

- Home Run Baker of the A's holds out all season and is then sold to the Yankees for $35,000.

- The Yankees wear pinstripes for the first time.

- Boston's Babe Ruth hits his first home run in the majors off the Yankees' Jack Warhop. He finishes the season with 18 wins, a .315 batting average, and four homers.

- The Cleveland team becomes known as the Indians.

> **"That's the first thing I can remember about him—the sound when he'd get a hold of one. It was just different, that's all."**
>
> —*Larry Gardner, reminiscing about Babe Ruth*

- Joe Jackson is traded from Cleveland to the Chicago White Sox.

- The Chalmers Award is discontinued, ending MVP selections until the 1920s.

- The Federal League folds after the season, with Chicago having edged St. Louis and Pittsburgh for the final pennant.

- The A's tumble to last place with a 43-109 record, down an all-time record 56 wins from the previous season.

- The Phillies climb from sixth place to first in one season, winning the NL by seven games with a 90-62 mark. It's the team's first pennant.

- Boston takes the AL flag by holding off Detroit, then wins the World Series in five games. Harry Hooper hits two short home runs in Game 5, and Rube Foster finishes the fall classic with two complete-game wins.

On April 24, Hack Cady becomes the last man to pinch-hit for Babe Ruth.

1916

Trades send Speaker, Mathewson packing... Ruth mows down opposition... Giants win 26 in a row

- Tris Speaker, traded from Boston to Cleveland after a salary dispute, leads the AL in BA (.386), SA (.502), hits (211), and doubles (41).

- Cincinnati's Hal Chase leads the NL in BA (.339) and hits (184).

- Phillie Pete Alexander tops the NL in complete games (38), ERA (1.55), wins (33), Ks (167), and shutouts (16—an all-time ML record).

- Washington's Walter Johnson leads the AL in wins (25), complete games (36), and Ks (228).

- Red Sox Babe Ruth wins 23 games and tops the AL in ERA (1.75) and shutouts (nine).

- The Giants lose eight straight home games to start the season, but they later win a record 26 games in a row—all at home.

> Cleveland's Marty Kavanagh hits the first pinch grand slam in AL history on September 24, when his blow skips through a hole in the fence.

- Detroit's Sam Crawford collects his ML-record 312th and last triple.

- On August 13, Ruth beats Johnson 1-0 in 13 innings.

- White Sox Joe Jackson leads the majors in triples (21) and total bases (293).

- The Cardinals pirate manager Branch Rickey from the crosstown Browns to run their front office.

- The Giants trade Christy Mathewson, Edd Roush, and Bill McKechnie to the Reds for Buck Herzog and Red Killefer. Mathewson replaces Herzog as Reds manager.

- Cubs owner Charlie Weeghman adopts the policy of allowing fans to keep balls hit into the stands.

- Brooklyn becomes the third NL team in succession to win its first pennant since 1901, nipping Philadelphia by 2½ games.

- The Red Sox finish two games ahead of Chicago in the AL, repeating as league champs. They also win their second straight World Series, again in five games. Ruth and Sherry Smith wage a 14-inning war in Game 2 before Boston prevails 2-1 in the best game of the set.

Pete Alexander

1917

Shore finishes what Ruth starts... Toney, Vaughn twirl no-hitters in stereo... White Sox go all the way

- Detroit's Ty Cobb leads the AL in BA (.383), SA (.571), hits (225), total bases (336), doubles (44), triples (23), and steals (55).

- Edd Roush of Cincinnati takes his first NL bat crown (.341).

- Cardinal Rogers Hornsby tops the NL in total bases (253), triples (17), and SA (.484).

- Phillie Pete Alexander leads the NL in wins (30), Ks (201), complete games (35), shutouts (eight), and innings (388).

- White Sox Eddie Cicotte tops the AL in wins (28) and ERA (1.53). His season includes a no-hitter over the Browns.

- The Pirates hire Hugo Bedzek, a college football coach, as their manager.

Eddie Cicotte

- Cincinnati's Fred Toney and Chicago's Hippo Vaughn toss no-hitters against each other on May 2, though Vaughn loses his in the 10th.

- Red Sox Ernie Shore pitches a controversial perfect game on June 23. Babe Ruth started on the mound, walked the first batter, and was ejected for arguing the call. Shore relieves and retires 27 straight batters.

- New York's Wally Pipp repeats as the AL's home run leader (nine). Dave Robertson and Gavvy Cravath tie for the NL title (12).

- Christy Mathewson, in his only full season as manager, steers the Reds to fourth place.

- Earned-run average becomes an official statistic in both leagues.

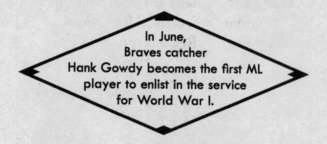

In June, Braves catcher Hank Gowdy becomes the first ML player to enlist in the service for World War I.

- In the Western Association, Ernie Calbert launches 43 home runs for Muskogee. The highest modern major-league total to this date was 24, set by Cravath in 1915.

- The White Sox win 100 games and the AL flag, their first since 1906.

- The Giants return to the top in the NL, running away from the Phillies by 10 games.

- Heinie Zimmerman's botched rundown in Game 6 of the World Series chases home a run and helps the White Sox to the world title. Red Faber pitches Chicago to three of its four wins.

1918

War effort shortens season, claims life of Grant... Several enlist, others drafted... Red Sox return to top

- Owing to World War I, the season ends on Labor Day, September 2.

- The majority of the minor leagues shut down in midseason due to the war.

- Detroit's Ty Cobb leads the AL in BA (.382) and triples (14).

- Washington's Walter Johnson tops the majors in wins (23), Ks (162), ERA (1.27), and shutouts (eight).

- On August 1 vs. the Pirates, Brave Art Nehf pitches 20 scoreless innings before finally losing 2-0 in 21 innings.

- The Yankees set a record with eight sacrifices (six bunts and two flies) in a game against Ruth and the Red Sox.

- Brooklyn's Zach Wheat wins the NL bat crown (.335).

- Chicago's Hippo Vaughn tops the NL in wins (22), ERA (1.74), and Ks (148).

- Red Sox Babe Ruth (13-7, 2.22 ERA) also leads the AL in SA (.555) and homers (11).

> **"Baseball received a knockout wallop yesterday when Secretary Baker ruled... [that] players in the draft age must obtain employment calculated to aid in the successful prosecution of the war or shoulder guns and fight."**
>
> —The Washington Star, *July 21*

- John K. Tener resigns after five years as president of the NL.

- The White Sox and Giants lose several players to the war and, as a result, fail to defend their titles. The Red Sox reclaim the AL, while the Cubs are a runaway winner of the NL pennant.

- Several players are drafted or enlist to aid the war effort, including Cincinnati manager Christy Mathewson. While in service, Mathewson is accidentally gassed and subsequently contracts tuberculosis.

- The Red Sox defeat Chicago in a six-game World Series that's played in just seven days.

- Players strike before Game 5, wanting higher World Series shares, but back off their stance and resume play.

- After "war reductions," members of the Red Sox receive $890 and members of the Cubs take home $535 in Series shares.

- Ruth extends his Series scoreless streak to 29⅔ innings.

- Former big-league infielder Eddie Grant, 35, is killed in action on October 5 in France. Known as Harvard Eddie, he's the only major-leaguer killed in World War I.

> The war-shortened season results in Cleveland playing 11 more road games than Boston does. Cleveland loses the AL pennant to the Red Sox by a game and a half.

1919

Babe enjoys first true "Ruthian" season... Johnson an Opening Day legend... Scandalous Sox hand Series to Reds

- The season is abbreviated to 140 games because of the war.

- Washington's Walter Johnson leads the AL in ERA (1.49), Ks (147), and shutouts (seven). He also sets a record by pitching his fifth consecutive Opening Day shutout.

- Red Sox Babe Ruth hits an ML-record 29 homers and tops the AL in runs (103), RBI (114), SA (.657), OBP (.456), and total bases (284).

- Ruth becomes the first to hit four grand slams in a season.

- Cincinnati's Edd Roush wins his second NL bat crown (.321).

- Detroit's Ty Cobb wins his final AL bat crown (.384).

- On September 28, the Giants beat the Phils 6-1 in an ML-record 51 minutes.

- White Sox Eddie Cicotte tops the ML in wins (29) and winning pct. (.806).

- Brooklyn's Hy Myers tops the NL in RBI (73), SA (.436), and total bases (223).

- Joe Wilhoit of Wichita (Western League) hits in 69 consecutive games.

> **"One thing that's always overlooked in the whole mess is that we could have beaten them no matter what the circumstances."**
>
> —*Edd Roush, referring to the Reds' tainted Series win over the White Sox*

- Pete Alexander returns to the game with the Cubs and leads the NL with a 1.72 ERA.

- The White Sox, behind Cicotte's pitching and Joe Jackson's .351 average and 96 RBI, win the AL pennant.

- The Reds compile a 96-44 record and win their first NL flag by nine games over New York.

- The World Series is extended to a best-of-nine affair to gain extra revenue, and the Reds win in eight.

- Suspicions are raised that members of the White Sox may have thrown the Series.

- Jackson, one of the players under suspicion, leads all Series performers with 12 hits and a .375 batting average.

- Lefty Williams, a 23-game winner during the season and another of the White Sox players under suspicion, sets a Series record for losses with three in as many starts.

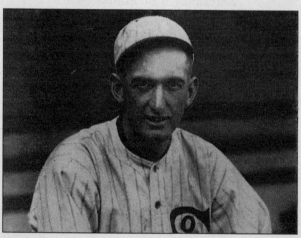

Joe Jackson

1920

Boston sells its Babe... Landis boots eight "Black Sox" from baseball... Cleveland reaches pinnacle

- In January, the Red Sox sell Babe Ruth to the Yankees for $125,000. Ruth responds by setting ML records for homers (54), runs (158), and slugging (.847).

- Late in the season, eight members of the White Sox are suspended for allegedly dumping the 1919 World Series. Eventually, these players are found innocent of rigging the Series by a Chicago jury. Nevertheless, Judge Kenesaw Mountain Landis permanently bars the eight players from organized baseball. Joe Jackson, Ed Cicotte, and Lefty Williams are among the "eight men out."

- Washington's Walter Johnson wins his 300th game.

- Cleveland shortstop Ray Chapman is beaned by New York pitcher Carl Mays on August 16 and dies the next day.

- Rube Foster organizes the Negro National League.

- St. Louis's George Sisler wins the AL bat title with a .407 average. He sets an ML record with 257 hits.

- St. Louis's Rogers Hornsby cops his first NL bat title (.370). He tops the league in hits (218), doubles (44), total bases (329), and SA (.559) and ties for the RBI crown (94).

- Jim Bagby of Cleveland is the last AL right-hander until 1968 to win 30 games in a season.

- The spitball and all other similar pitches are abolished.

- On October 2, Pittsburgh and Cincinnati play the last ML tripleheader.

- On May 1, Leon Cadore of Brooklyn and Joe Oeschger of Boston both pitch all 26 innings of a 1-1 tie.

- Cleveland's Tris Speaker sets a new ML record with 11 consecutive base hits.

- Chicago's Pete Alexander heads the NL in wins (27), ERA (1.91), complete games (33), innings (363), and strikeouts (173).

- Cleveland beats the White Sox by two games to win its first AL pennant.

Babe Ruth

- The Brooklyn Robins finish 93-61, seven games ahead of the Giants in the race for the NL flag.

- In Game 5 of the World Series, Cleveland second baseman Bill Wambsganss makes an unassisted triple play—a Series first. He also hits into a double play, accounting for five outs on two pitches.

- Cleveland wins the Series five games to two, with a pitching staff that posts a microscopic 0.89 ERA. Stan Coveleski wins three games on a total of only 261 pitches.

Ruth redefines power hitting... Baseball graces the airwaves... Giants outlast Yankees in "Subway Series"

- Yankee Babe Ruth clubs 59 homers to shatter his own year-old record, and, in the process, hits his 137th career homer, breaking Roger Connor's mark of 136. Ruth also sets an ML RBI record with 171. In addition to producing an all-time ML-record 457 total bases, he scores 177 runs, a 20th-century record.

- Rogers Hornsby, now installed at second for the Cards, cops his second NL bat crown at .397. He tops the NL in hits (235), RBI (126), runs (131), doubles (44), and total bases (378). He also leads in runs produced (236), OBP (.458), and SA (.639) and ties in triples (18).

- Detroit's Harry Heilmann hits .394 to win his first AL bat title. He also leads in hits (237).

- Chewing gum magnate William Wrigley buys the Cubs.

- Yank Carl Mays leads the AL in winning pct. (.750), innings (337), and games (49) and ties for the lead in wins (27) and saves (seven).

- The introduction of a livelier ball results in the Tigers hitting .316 as a team, an AL record. The AL as a whole hits a league-record .292.

- Red Faber's AL-leading 2.48 ERA is the only ERA below 3.00 in that circuit. Faber and teammate Dickie Kerr account for 44 of the White Sox's 62 victories.

- On August 5, Harold Arlin of radio station KDKA in Pittsburgh does the first broadcast of a baseball game.

- On April 28, Cleveland pitcher George Uhle collects six RBI in a game.

- The game's moguls rule that 17 pitchers can continue to use the spitball for the rest of their careers.

- Specs Toporcer of the Cards is the first infielder in ML history to wear glasses.

- Red Sox Stuffy McInnis's .999 fielding average is an ML record for first basemen.

- Brooklyn's Burleigh Grimes leads the NL in complete games (30) and Ks (136), and he ties for the lead in wins (22).

- Detroit's Ty Cobb collects his 3,000th hit at the age of 34.

- The Browns' Jack Tobin, George Sisler, and Baby Doll Jacobson all collect more than 200 hits.

- The Yankees capture their first of many AL pennants, leaving only the Senators and Browns searching for their inaugural flags.

> **"When I hit a ball, I want someone else to go chase it."**
>
> —*Cardinal Rogers Hornsby, on why he preferred baseball to golf*

- The Giants return to the top in the NL by a four-game margin over Pittsburgh, giving manager John McGraw his seventh pennant and setting up the first true "Subway Series."

- Overcoming a 2-0 deficit, the Giants defeat Ruth and the Yankees in eight games. Waite Hoyt of the Yanks wins two games and posts an ERA of 0.00 in three starts, but he loses the finale 1-0.

1922

Hornsby tops .400 mark... Ruth slips to 35 homers in partial season... Giants frustrate Yanks again

- Suspended part of the season for an illegal barnstorming tour the previous fall, the Yankees' Babe Ruth drops to 35 homers.

- The AL gives out a league MVP Award for the first time. George Sisler of the Browns wins handily. Sisler leads the AL with a .420 BA. He also hits in 41 straight games, an AL record.

- Eddie Rommel of the seventh-place A's leads the AL with 27 wins.

- Detroit's Harry Heilmann hits 21 homers. Ten of them come in Shibe Park against the A's.

- On August 25, the Cubs beat the Phils 26-23 in the highest-scoring game in ML history.

- Ray Grimes of the Cubs drives in at least one run in an ML-record 17 straight games.

George Sisler

- White Sox owner Charlie Comiskey forks over $125,000 to San Francisco of the Pacific Coast League for Willie Kamm.

- Ken Williams of the Browns becomes the new AL homer king (39). Williams also leads in RBI (155), total bases (367), and runs produced (244). On April 22, he becomes the first player since 1897 to hit three homers in a game.

- St. Louis's Rogers Hornsby sets post-1900 NL records with 42 homers, 152 RBI, and a .722 slugging average. His .401 BA makes him the first NLer in the 20th century to top the .400 mark. Hornsby hits in 33 straight games.

- The Supreme Court rules that baseball is a sport, not a business, and not subject to antitrust laws.

- Pittsburgh's Max Carey sets a stolen-base percentage record of .962 when he's successful in 51 of 53 attempts. Carey steals a record (since broken) 31 consecutive bases.

- On April 30, White Sox Charlie Robertson tosses a perfect game vs. Detroit.

- Chicago's Red Faber tops the AL in ERA (2.80), complete games (31), and innings (353).

- The Yankees, playing without the suspended Ruth and Bob Meusel for the first month of the season, have to come from behind to beat the Browns by one game for the AL pennant.

> **"Kenneth Williams was the stalwart figure who picked up the king's idle bludgeon in the true kingly fashion."**
>
> —Baseball Magazine, *reviewing the 1922 season*

- The Giants repeat by seven games in the NL, this time over Cincinnati, with pitcher Eppa Rixey leading the league in wins (25).

- The second "Subway Series" is much shorter than the first, with the Giants prevailing in a four-game sweep (plus one tie). They hold the Yankees to 11 runs in five games. Ruth hits just .118.

1923

Ruth bats .393, takes home first MVP trophy... Yankee Stadium opens... Yanks turn tables on Giants

- New York's Babe Ruth is selected the AL's MVP. Ruth regains the AL homer crown by belting 41. Among his other notable achievements for the year, he reaches base an all-time record 379 times and collects a record 170 walks. Ruth is the AL runner-up in batting with a .393 BA, his personal best. His .545 OBP sets an ML record.

- Rogers Hornsby of St. Louis takes his fourth consecutive NL bat crown (.384).

- Detroit's Harry Heilmann begins his odd knack for copping the AL bat crown every other year as he hits .403.

- Cy Williams of the Phillies hits 41 homers to top the NL.

- Cleveland's Tris Speaker sets a modern record for doubles with 59.

- Yankee Stadium opens on April 18. New York wins 4-1 over Boston on a three-run homer by Ruth.

- Detroit's Ty Cobb scores his 1,736th run, moving ahead of Honus Wagner on the all-time list.

- The Yankees collect an AL-record 30 hits vs. Boston on September 28.

- On July 7 vs. Boston, Cleveland scores 13 runs in the sixth and wins 27-3.

- Giants pitcher Jack Bentley hits .427 in 89 at-bats.

- On August 24, Yankee Carl Mays beats the A's for an AL-record 23rd consecutive time.

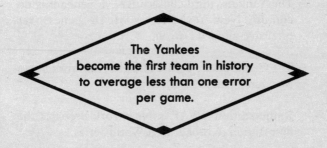

The Yankees become the first team in history to average less than one error per game.

- Red Sox first baseman George Burns performs an unassisted triple play on September 14. Braves shortstop Ernie Padgett performs an unassisted triple play on October 6.

- Yankee Everett Scott leads AL shortstops in fielding average for the eighth consecutive year.

- Paul Strand of Salt Lake City in the PCL collects an organized-baseball record 325 hits in a season.

- Pete Schneider of Vernon in the PCL hits five homers and a double in one game.

- Giant Frankie Frisch leads the NL in hits (223), total bases (311), and runs produced (215).

- George Kelly of the Giants becomes the first major-leaguer to homer in three successive innings, going deep in the third, fourth, and fifth of a 13-6 win at Wrigley Field.

- The Yankees' third consecutive AL pennant is no contest. New York cruises by 16 games over offensive-minded Detroit.

- The Giants assure a third straight New York Series by winning another NL flag.

- Radio station WEAF in New York becomes the first station to broadcast a World Series.

- This time, the Yankees get the upper hand in the fall classic, beating the Giants in six games. Ruth homers into the upper deck at the Polo Grounds in the final game.

1924

Vance first to win NL MVP... Senators spell relief "F-I-R-P-O"... Washington prevails in Series thriller

- Washington's Walter Johnson wins the AL MVP Award. Johnson's 23 wins and 158 strikeouts pace the AL. He also leads in ERA (2.72), winning pct. (.767), and shutouts (six). Johnson's AL strikeout crown is his record 12th.

- The NL joins the AL in giving a league MVP Award. The first NL winner is Brooklyn's Dazzy Vance. Vance leads the majors in wins with 28, Ks with 262, and ERA at 2.16.

- St. Louis's Rogers Hornsby leads the NL with a .424 BA, a post-1900 ML record. He tops the NL in hits (227), doubles (43), walks (89), total bases (373), and SA (.696) and ties in runs (121).

- New York's Babe Ruth tops the AL in homers (46) and BA (.378). Although he tops the majors in runs (143), walks (142), OBP (.513), SA (.739), and total bases (391), Ruth fails to win the Triple

Rogers Hornsby

Crown when he finishes second in RBI to Washington's Goose Goslin, 129 to 121.

- Washington's Firpo Marberry (15 saves) becomes the first relief specialist in ML history.

- Jim Bottomley of the Cards collects an ML-record 12 RBI in a September 16 game vs. Brooklyn.

- Giant Heinie Groh's .983 fielding average sets an ML record for third basemen.

- The Giants' Jimmy O'Connell is banned from baseball for offering an oral bribe to a Phils player on the last weekend of the season.

- On August 2, Joe Hauser of the A's sets an AL record with 14 total bases in a game.

- Sam Rice of Washington hits in 31 consecutive games.

- Lyman Lamb of Tulsa in the Western League hits an organized-baseball record 100 doubles.

- WMAQ in Chicago broadcasts the home games of both the Cubs and the White Sox.

- Giants manager John McGraw wins his NL-record 10th and last pennant. His troops receive a surprising challenge from Brooklyn before narrowly holding off the Dodgers and Pittsburgh.

- There's a new AL champion when the Yankees' pitching falters. Johnson, finally pitching for a Washington team that gives him offensive support, hurls the Senators to their first flag.

- Johnson loses two Series starts to the Giants, but he wins the seventh and deciding game in a relief role. He pitches the final four frames of a 4-3, 12-inning marathon that stands out as one of the most exciting finishes in Series history.

Hornsby cops second Triple Crown... Collins, Speaker join 3,000-hit club... Gehrig becomes a regular

- Babe Ruth's famous "bellyache" idles him for much of the season, holding him to a .290 BA and 25 homers. The Yankees tumble to seventh place.

- St. Louis's Rogers Hornsby is selected the NL MVP. He wins his sixth straight NL bat crown (.403) and his second Triple Crown, leading in homers (39) and RBI (143). He also leads the majors in SA (.756), runs produced (237), and OBP (.489). Hornsby's SA sets an NL record.

- Washington shortstop Roger Peckinpaugh wins the AL MVP Award, even though he commits eight errors in the World Series.

- Bob Meusel, Ruth's New York teammate, leads the AL in homers (33) and RBI (138).

- Detroit's Harry Heilmann wins the AL bat crown at .393.

- Brooklyn's Dazzy Vance leads the majors with 22 wins and 221 Ks.

- Joe Sewell of Cleveland fans just four times in 608 at-bats.

- George Burns of the Reds steals home for the 27th time, setting an NL career record.

- Washington's Sam Rice collects an AL-record 182 singles.

> **"He could throw a cream puff through a battleship."**
>
> —*Johnny Frederick on Brooklyn's Dazzy Vance*

- The Senators' Walter Johnson hits .433, a season record for pitchers with 75-plus at-bats.

- Tony Lazzeri of Salt Lake City in the PCL hits 60 homers, a new organized-baseball record.

- The Browns' George Sisler hits in 34 straight games to begin the season.

- Eddie Collins of the White Sox and Cleveland's Tris Speaker each collect their 3,000th hit.

- Pittsburgh's Max Carey tops the NL in steals for a record 10th time.

- Philly's Al Simmons collects 253 hits, an AL record for outfielders.

- On May 5 in St. Louis, Detroit's Ty Cobb goes 6-for-6 with three homers and 16 total bases.

- Yankee Everett Scott's streak of 1,307 consecutive games played ends. Lou Gehrig starts a skein of 2,130 consecutive games.

- Pittsburgh's Glenn Wright performs an unassisted triple play on May 7.

- Former pitching great Christy Mathewson dies from tuberculosis.

- Washington successfully defends its AL pennant, with no competition from the Yankees. A rebuilding A's team finishes second.

- Pittsburgh ends the Giants' string of four straight NL pennants, winning their first since 1909 and becoming the first team in history to score 900 runs.

- In a reversal of the 1924 Series, Johnson wins two games but loses the seventh. Pittsburgh wins the deciding contest 9-7, gaining a championship that was helped along by Peckinpaugh and his eight Senator errors at shortstop.

1926

Ruth regains his dominant swing... Phils overcome Babe's Series blasts... O'Farrell, Burns named top players

- Cards catcher Bob O'Farrell wins the NL MVP Award.

- George Burns of Cleveland takes the AL MVP prize. Burns sets an ML record with 64 doubles and hits .358.

- Cincinnati's Bubbles Hargrave breaks Rogers Hornsby's stranglehold on the NL bat title, winning with a .353 average.

- Cleveland's George Uhle leads the majors with 27 wins.

- Philly's Lefty Grove wins his first AL ERA crown (2.51) and again tops the loop in Ks (194).

- On August 28, Dutch Levsen of Cleveland becomes the last pitcher to win two complete games in one day.

- Firpo Marberry has 22 saves for Washington, an ML record.

- Detroit's Heinie Manush takes the AL bat crown (.378).

- Hack Wilson of the Cubs wins his first NL home run crown (21).

- Yankee Babe Ruth tops the AL in homers with 47, 26 more than anyone else. He also leads in runs (139), total bases (365), SA (.737), OBP (.516), RBI (145), walks (144), and runs produced (237).

> **"He was frank to the point of being cruel, and subtle as a belch."**
>
> —Lee Allen, *describing Rogers Hornsby*

- St. Louis's Jim Bottomley tops the NL in RBI (120), doubles (40), and total bases (305).

- In his first full season as the Cards' player/manager, Hornsby slumps to .317.

- The Red Sox finish last in the AL and lose a club-record 107 games.

- Giant Mel Ott, age 17, becomes the youngest player to get a pinch hit in NL history.

- On September 26, the Browns and Yankees play the shortest game in AL history—55 minutes. On the same day, the two teams play the shortest doubleheader in ML history—two hours and seven minutes.

- On August 15, Babe Herman doubles into a double play as three Dodgers wind up on third base.

- In Hornsby's first full season at the controls, the Cardinals bring St. Louis its first pennant in a half-century of competition in the NL. Their two-game margin over Cincinnati gives the city its first championship of any kind since the Browns of the American Association won in 1888.

- The AL flag goes to the Yankees, who jump from seventh place in 1925 to claim their fourth pennant of the decade.

- Ruth hits a World Series single-game record three homers in Game 4 and a record four home runs overall, but it's the Cardinals who prevail. Down three games to two, St. Louis wins the final pair. Pete Alexander's relief pitching stymies the Yanks in the final game.

- On December 20, the Cards deal player/manager Hornsby to the Giants for Frankie Frisch and Jimmy Ring.

1927

"Murderer's Row" terrorizes opposing pitchers... Ruth cracks 60 homers... Cobb reaches 4,000 career hits

- Yankee Lou Gehrig is selected the AL MVP. His 175 RBI set an ML record (since broken). Gehrig hits 47 homers, giving him and Babe Ruth a teammate-record 107 that will stand until 1961.

- Ruth slugs an ML-record 60 home runs (since broken). Ruth himself hits more homers than every other team in the AL except his own. He leads the majors in runs (158), walks (138), SA (.772), and OBP (.487).

- Cub Charlie Root tops the majors in wins with 26.

- Wilcy Moore wins 19 games for the Yankees and ties for the AL lead in saves (13). Moore leads the majors in ERA (2.28).

- For the fourth odd year in succession, Detroit's Harry Heilmann takes the AL bat title (.398).

Lou Gehrig and Babe Ruth

- Pirates rookie Lloyd Waner hits 198 singles and collects an ML rookie-record 223 hits. Paul Waner, teammate and brother of Lloyd, is the NL MVP. He leads the NL in batting (.380), hits (237), triples (17), total bases (338), and RBI (131). The Waner brothers hit a combined .367 with 460 hits—both ML season sibling records.

- The Yankees score an ML-record 975 runs (since broken).

- Ty Cobb signs with the A's prior to the season after 22 years with Detroit. Cobb gets his 4,000th hit on July 19, off Detroit's Sam Gibson.

- Commissioner Kenesaw Mountain Landis "permits" Cobb and Tris Speaker to resign from their clubs after being accused of fixing a 1919 game between Detroit and Cleveland. Each joins a new team, and AL president Ban Johnson is forced to resign for publicly protesting the decision.

- Walter Johnson retires with an ML-record 3,508 Ks (since broken). Johnson's 110 shutouts are an all-time ML record.

- On May 17, the Braves' Bob Smith pitches a 22-inning complete game, losing 4-3 to the Cubs.

- On May 30, Cubs shortstop Jimmy Cooney makes an unassisted triple play. The following day, Tigers first baseman Johnny Neun also turns the trick.

- Giant Rogers Hornsby tops the NL in walks (86), OBP (.448), and runs (133).

- The Yankees win 110 games, winning the AL by 19. The NL has a three-team pennant race, with Pittsburgh the late-season winner.

- New York sweeps the World Series, outscoring Pittsburgh 23-10 in four days with a lineup that forever becomes known as "Murderer's Row." Ruth bats .400 and drives in seven runs.

1928

Cobb, Speaker hang up their cleats... Cubs' Wilson keeps hacking... Gehrig, Ruth help Yanks dominate Series

- Jim Bottomley of the Cards is named NL MVP.

- Philly catcher Mickey Cochrane wins the AL MVP by two votes over St. Louis's Heinie Manush.

- Rogers Hornsby, playing now for the Braves, tops the NL in batting (.387).

- Washington's Goose Goslin wins the AL bat crown (.379) by one point over Manush.

- Manush tops the AL in hits (241) and ties in doubles (47).

- Cub Hack Wilson again ties for the NL homer crown (31), this time with Bottomley.

- Dodger Dazzy Vance's 2.09 ERA is the best in the majors. Vance wins 22 games, tops the NL in shutouts (four), and leads the majors in Ks (200).

- Yankee Babe Ruth tops the majors in homers (54), runs (163), walks (135), and SA (.709). Ruth and teammate Lou Gehrig tie for the ML lead in RBI with 142.

- Giant Larry Benton ties for the most wins in the ML (25) and leads the NL in winning pct. (.735).

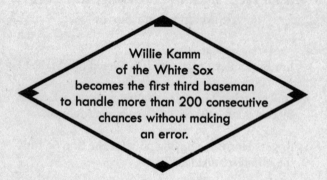

Willie Kamm of the White Sox becomes the first third baseman to handle more than 200 consecutive chances without making an error.

- Ty Cobb retires with ML records for BA (.367) and runs scored (2,245) (records still stand). In addition, he retires with ML records in hits (4,191), stolen bases (892), and RBI (1,961) (all since broken).

- Tris Speaker retires as the all-time ML leader in doubles (792) and assists by an outfielder (448).

- Eddie Collins plays the last of his career-record 2,650 games at second base.

- Giant Freddy Lindstrom's 231 hits set an NL record for third basemen and top the senior loop.

- The last-place Phils have a 5.52 staff ERA, a new ML high.

- Taylor Douthit of the Cards handles 566 chances, an all-time ML record for an outfielder.

- The Yankees sweep the A's in a key three-game AL series late in the season, and two weeks later clinch another pennant.

- Bill McKechnie, who managed the 1925 Pirates to the pennant, guides the Cardinals to their second flag in three years. The Giants finish two games back.

- The most one-sided Series in history goes once again to the Yankees. The four-game run differential is 27-10, with Ruth and Gehrig leading the way for New York. The closest game is a 4-1 Series opener.

- Ruth hits .625 in the World Series to set a Series BA record. Gehrig hits .545 and has a 1.727 SA, an all-time World Series record. Between them, Ruth and Gehrig hit seven homers and knock in 13 runs.

- The Braves, after one season with Hornsby, trade him to the Cubs for five players and $200,000.

1929

Yankees lose manager Huggins... New uniform, same result for Hornsby... A's ride 10-run inning to Series victory

- Rogers Hornsby of the Cubs wins the NL MVP (the AL discontinued the award after the 1928 season). Hornsby's .380 BA sets a Cubs team record—the fourth such record he has set in the decade.

- Chuck Klein of the Phils wins the NL homer crown (43) in his first full season.

- Yankee Babe Ruth tops the majors with 46 homers and a .697 SA.

- George Earnshaw of the A's leads the majors with 24 wins.

- Cub Hack Wilson's 159 RBI are the most in the majors.

- Lefty Grove of the A's posts a 2.81 ERA, the only one in the majors below 3.00.

- Lefty O'Doul of the Phils, the NL bat champ with a .398 mark, is the MVP runner-up. O'Doul's 254 hits tie the all-time NL record. He also reaches base an NL-record 334 times.

- Yankees manager Miller Huggins dies near the end of the season.

- Giant Mel Ott, age 20, becomes the youngest player ever to hit 40 homers in a season; he hits 42.

- Braves owner Emil "Judge" Fuchs manages his own team for the full season—the last owner to do so.

- Ike Boone of the Mission Reds in the PCL collects 553 total bases.

- Johnny Frederick of Brooklyn sets an ML rookie record with 52 doubles.

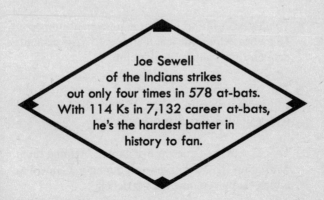

Joe Sewell of the Indians strikes out only four times in 578 at-bats. With 114 Ks in 7,132 career at-bats, he's the hardest batter in history to fan.

- The Phils are the only team in NL history to have four 200-hit men.

- Dale Alexander of Detroit collects 215 hits, setting an AL rookie record for a 154-game season.

- Philly's Al Simmons leads the AL in total bases (373), RBI (157), and runs produced (237).

- Detroit's Charlie Gehringer tops the AL in runs (131), triples (19), steals (28), and hits (215).

- The Indians and Yankees become the first teams to put numbers on their uniforms and keep them on.

- On July 5, the Giants become the first ML team to use a public address system.

- New York's Bill Walker leads the NL in ERA at 3.08, the highest NL-leading mark of the century.

- The Yankees fail to win the AL pennant, finishing 18 games behind the A's. It ends a 15-year pennant drought for Connie Mack's club.

- The NL pennant race is also a breeze, with the Cubs coming out on top. Their 98-54 record wraps up their first flag since 1918.

- The A's win the Series in five games. Helping them wrap it up is a 10-run seventh inning in Game 4 in which they overcome an 8-0 deficit.

Runs are up all over... Wilson amasses 190 RBI... A's repeat as world champs

- The Cubs' Hack Wilson is named NL MVP after driving in an ML-record 190 runs. Wilson also sets an NL record with 56 home runs.

- Dodger Dazzy Vance's 2.61 ERA is 1.15 runs better than the next-lowest ERA in the NL.

- Lefty Grove of the A's leads the majors in wins (28), winning pct. (.848), Ks (209), and, amazingly, saves (nine). Grove's 2.54 ERA is .77 runs better than the next-lowest ERA in the AL.

- Al Simmons of the A's tops the AL in batting (.381), runs (152), and runs produced (281).

- Giant Bill Terry leads the NL with a .401 BA, the last .400 average in the league.

- Cub Gabby Hartnett's .630 SA sets an ML record for catchers.

Hack Wilson

- After a long holdout, Babe Ruth signs for $80,000—an ML-record salary at this juncture. While Ruth leads the AL with 49 homers, he also becomes the first documented player to fan 1,000 times in his career.

- Philly's Chuck Klein scores 158 runs, a 20th-century NL record. Klein also tops the NL in doubles (59) and runs produced (288). The latter sets an NL record.

- Cincy's Harry Heilmann becomes the first player to homer in every major-league park in use during his career.

- On May 6, Gene Rye of Waco in the Texas League hits three home runs in one inning.

- At age 46, Jack Quinn of the A's becomes the oldest player to homer in an ML game.

- Cardinal George Watkins sets an ML rookie record when he hits .373.

- Brave Wally Berger sets NL rookie records with 38 homers and 119 RBI.

- Senator Sam Rice's 207 hits, 121 runs, and 271 total bases all set records for a player over age 40.

- Yankee Lou Gehrig tops the AL in total bases (419) and RBI (174).

- The Yankees set an ML record with 1,062 runs.

- The A's ride the slugging of Simmons and Jimmie Foxx to a repeat AL pennant. The two combine for 73 home runs and 321 RBI.

- The Cardinals are victorious by two games over the Cubs in the NL, with a lineup that has all eight hitters over the .300 mark.

- Philadelphia records a second consecutive World Series triumph in six games. The A's get two wins apiece from Grove and George Earnshaw.

1931

Grove, Frisch win first BBWAA MVP Awards... Gehrig, Ruth share home run crown... Cards go seven to beat A's

- The Baseball Writers Association of America appoints two committees, one in each league, to elect the MVPs.

- Lefty Grove is selected as the first BBWAA winner in the AL. Grove tops the majors in wins (31), Ks (175), winning pct. (.886), and ERA (2.06), and he ties in complete games (27). He wins 16 straight games during the season, tying an AL record.

- Frankie Frisch of the Cards wins the MVP Award in the NL.

- Phillie Chuck Klein tops the NL in homers with 31 and RBI with 121.

- No NL pitcher wins 20 games—the first time that's happened in ML history. The AL's Grove, in contrast, becomes the last southpaw of the 20th century to win 30 games in a season.

- Cardinal Chick Hafey wins the batting title at .349, slightly better than Giant Bill Terry, who also hits .349.

- Yankee Lou Gehrig totals an ML-record 301 runs produced. Gehrig tallies an AL-record 184 RBI. He also tops the AL in hits (211), runs (163), and total bases (410).

- Babe Ruth wins his last home run crown by tying with teammate Gehrig for the title (46).

- Bill Walker of the Giants wins his second NL ERA title (2.26).

Lefty Grove

- The Yankees have six men who score 100 or more runs. The team scores an ML-record 1,067 runs.

- Joe McCarthy, fired the previous year by the Cubs, becomes manager of the Yankees.

- Cleveland's Wes Ferrell hits a season-record nine home runs while serving as a pitcher.

- The AL rules that all teams must have numbers on their uniforms.

- The sacrifice fly rule is abolished. Balls bouncing over or going through a fence, heretofore considered home runs, are now ruled doubles.

- Earl Webb of the Red Sox hits an ML-record 67 doubles.

- Negro League star Josh Gibson reportedly hits 75 home runs for the Homestead Grays.

- Only New York and Washington finish within 30 games of the A's, who go 107-45.

- Frisch's sensational year ignites the Cardinals to a 101-53 record and the NL pennant.

- For the second straight year, Grove and George Earnshaw pitch fabulously for the A's in the Series, but the Cards prevail in seven games. Pepper Martin bats .500 for the winners.

1932

Rookie Dean wows, whiffs batters... McCarthy steers Yanks to pinnacle... Ruth's Series shot: Called?

- Philly's Jimmie Foxx is selected AL MVP. Foxx leads the AL in homers (58), RBI (169), SA (.749), runs (151), and total bases (438). His 58 homers are the most at this juncture by anyone other than Babe Ruth.

- Philly's Chuck Klein is the NL MVP. Klein ties for the homer crown (38) and leads the NL in runs produced (251).

- Al Crowder of Washington tops the majors with 26 wins.

- John McGraw steps down as Giants manager after 40 games and turns the reins over to player Bill Terry.

- After the 1932 season, the A's sell Al Simmons, Jimmy Dykes, and Mule Haas to the White Sox for $100,000.

Ruth's called shot

- The Red Sox again tumble into the cellar and set a new club record for losses with 111.

- St. Louis rookie Dizzy Dean tops the NL with 191 strikeouts.

- Lon Warneke of the Cubs is the NL's top winner with 22.

- Brooklyn's Lefty O'Doul wins his second NL bat crown in four years (.368).

- Pittsburgh's Paul Waner sets an NL record (since broken) with 62 doubles.

- New York's Mel Ott wins his first NL homer crown (38, tied with Klein).

- Brooklyn's Johnny Frederick hits an ML-record six pinch-hit home runs during the season.

- On June 3, Yankee Lou Gehrig becomes the first player in the 20th century to hit four home runs in a game.

- Philly's Don Hurst tops the NL in RBI with 143, a record for NL first basemen.

- On July 10, Ed Rommel of the A's gives up a record 29 hits and 14 runs in relief. Rommel also pitches an AL relief-record 17 innings in the game.

- On July 10, Johnny Burnett of Cleveland bangs out an ML-record nine hits.

- In his last great year, Ruth bats .341 with 120 runs, 137 RBI, and an AL-leading 130 walks.

- The Yankees win their first pennant under Joe McCarthy, finishing 107-47.

- The Cubs take the NL flag after Charlie Grimm replaces Rogers Hornsby as manager.

- The Yanks sweep the third World Series in a row in which they have appeared. Legend has it that Ruth "calls his shot" in Game 3 at Chicago.

- Gehrig leads all World Series hitters with a .529 BA, three homers, and eight RBI.

Hubbell nearly unhittable for Series-winning Giants... Foxx, Klein win Triple Crowns... All-Star Game debuts

- Giant pitcher Carl Hubbell wins the NL MVP vote. Hubbell's 1.66 ERA is the lowest ever by an NL lefty who pitches over 300 innings.

- Jimmie Foxx of the A's is named the AL MVP to become the first player ever to cop consecutive awards. Foxx takes the Triple Crown in the AL, batting .356 with 48 homers and 163 RBI. He also leads in SA (.703) and total bases (403).

- Lefty Grove of the A's and Washington's Al Crowder tie for the ML lead in wins with 24.

- In the first All-Star Game, the AL beats the NL 4-2 at Comiskey Park. Babe Ruth hits the first homer in All-Star competition—a two-run shot.

- Philly's Chuck Klein wins the Triple Crown in the NL, batting .368 with 28 homers and 120 RBI. He also leads the NL in hits (223), doubles (44), total bases (365), and runs produced (193). Klein sets a 20th-century NL record when he collects 200 hits for the fifth consecutive year. In November, the financially strapped Phillies send Klein to the Cubs for three second-line players and $65,000.

- Washington's Heinie Manush has a 33-game hitting streak.

- Ruth leads the AL for the last time in a major offensive department—walks with 114.

- Yankee Lou Gehrig surpasses Everett Scott's record streak of 1,307 consecutive games played.

> **"I never tried to outsmart nobody. It was easier to outdummy them."**
>
> —*The Cards' Dizzy Dean, to sportswriter Red Smith*

- Joe Hauser hits 69 home runs for Minneapolis of the American Association, becoming the first player in organized baseball to slug 60 twice in his career.

- Nick Altrock, age 57, pinch-hits in a game for Washington.

- On July 19, Dizzy Dean fans 17 Cubs, setting a modern ML record. Dean again tops the NL in Ks (199).

- On July 19, Wes and Rick Ferrell become the first pair of brothers on opposing teams to homer in the same game.

- Tom Yawkey buys the moribund Red Sox. The bank takes over the bankrupt Reds; Powell Crosley eventually buys the club.

- Commissioner Kenesaw Mountain Landis opens the season by taking a 40 percent pay cut because of the Great Depression.

- For the first time in three decades, a season begins without the fiery John McGraw in uniform. He had resigned during the previous campaign.

- Bill Terry, who took over for McGraw a year earlier, calls the shots as the Giants win their first NL flag since 1924.

- Shortstop Joe Cronin, with a league-leading 45 doubles, manages the Senators to the last pennant won by a Washington-based team in the majors. The fading Yankees finish seven games behind.

- Hubbell remains masterful as the Giants win the World Series in five games. The lefty pitches two complete-game victories without allowing an earned run.

1934

Dean machine turns tide in Series... Hubbell fans five straight legends... Ruth blasts 700th career homer

- The Cardinals' Dizzy Dean is selected the NL MVP. Dean leads the NL in winning pct. (.811), shutouts (seven), and Ks (195). He becomes the last NL hurler to win 30 games, winning 30 exactly.

- Detroit player/manager Mickey Cochrane is the AL MVP.

- New York's Lou Gehrig wins the Triple Crown in the AL, batting .363 with 49 homers and 165 RBI. He also leads in SA (.706) and total bases (409). Gehrig ties an AL record by leading the loop in RBI for a fifth time.

- Giant Carl Hubbell's 2.30 ERA is the best in the majors.

- In February, legendary ex-Giants manager John McGraw dies of prostate cancer at age 60.

- Paul Waner of Pittsburgh tops the NL in batting at .362. He also leads the NL in runs (122) and hits (217).

- Yankee Lefty Gomez leads the AL in wins (26), winning pct. (.839), Ks (158), complete games (25), ERA (2.33), and shutouts (six).

- In the All-Star Game, Hubbell fans Babe Ruth, Gehrig, Jimmie Foxx, Al Simmons, and Joe Cronin consecutively. The AL wins 9-7.

- The Yankees obtain prospect Joe DiMaggio from the PCL San Francisco Seals for $25,000 and five players.

> **"Dizzy talked. Paul listened. Dizzy wisecracked. Paul laughed. Dizzy was a great comedian. Paul was his best audience. Each was the other's hero."**
>
> —*J. Roy Stockton*

- Senators owner Clark Griffith sends his son-in-law, Cronin, to the Red Sox for Lyn Lary and $250,000.

- Hal Trosky of Cleveland collects 374 total bases, setting an ML rookie record.

- The Yankees' Ruth hits his 700th career homer.

- Reds players fly to a game in Chicago—the first ML teammates to travel together by air.

- On May 1, the Yankees' Burleigh Grimes wins the last game in ML history by a pitcher legally allowed to throw a spitball.

- Detroit's Schoolboy Rowe ties an AL record with 16 straight wins.

- New York's Mel Ott leads the NL in homers (35), RBI (135), and runs produced (219).

- Cardinal Ripper Collins tops the NL in total bases (369) and SA (.615) and ties in homers (35).

- Tiger Charlie Gehringer leads the AL in hits (214), runs (134), and runs produced (250).

- Detroit finishes the year with a .300 batting average, and it carries the Tigers to a 101-53 record and their first AL pennant since 1909.

- The "Gashouse Gang" Cardinals win the NL flag by two over the Giants.

- The Cardinals beat the Tigers in a Series that goes the distance. The Dean brothers, Dizzy and Paul, record two Series wins apiece for the Cards and record ERAs under 2.00.

1935

Ruth retires a Brave... Reds nip Phils under the lights... Cubs win 21 straight, lose to Tigers in Series

- Hank Greenberg wins the AL MVP Award. Greenberg's 170 RBI top the majors by 40 and the AL by 51. He also leads in total bases (389) and runs produced (255).

- Cubs catcher Gabby Hartnett is named NL MVP.

- Boston pitcher Wes Ferrell rebounds from a sore arm to top the AL in wins with 25.

- The Cardinals' Dizzy Dean again paces the NL in wins (28).

- Pittsburgh's Arky Vaughan tops the NL in hitting at .385.

- Released by the Yankees, Babe Ruth signs a three-year contract with the Braves. On May 25, Ruth hits three homers vs. Pittsburgh at Forbes Field. He retires a few days later.

- Ruth's 714th and final home run is said to have traveled 600 feet from home plate, clearing the right-field grandstand and the roof before exiting the stadium. It is the longest ever hit at Forbes Field.

- Ruth retires with a .690 career SA and 2,056 career walks (still ML records). Ruth also sets ML career records in homers (714), RBI (2,211), OBP (.474), and extra-base hits (1,356) (all since broken).

- Washington's Buddy Myer wins the AL batting title by a single point over Cleveland's Joe Vosmik (.349 to .348).

Hank Greenberg

- On May 24, the Reds beat the Phils 2-1 at Crosley Field in the first ML night game. On July 10, Cub Babe Herman hits the first homer in a night game.

- The Cubs win 21 straight games, setting an ML record for most consecutive wins without a tie.

- Philly's Jimmie Foxx leads in SA (.636) and ties Greenberg for the AL homer crown (36). After the season, the A's sell Foxx and Johnny Marcum to the Red Sox for $150,000.

- Despite having 110 RBI by the All-Star break, Greenberg is not picked for the AL team. The first basemen are Lou Gehrig and Foxx.

- Wally Berger of the cellar-dwelling Braves leads the NL in homers (34) and RBI (130).

- The Braves finish with an NL-record 115 losses.

- The Cubs, thanks to their 21-game surge, overtake the Cardinals and win the NL pennant by four games with a 100-win season.

- The Tigers hold off the Yankees by three games to win the AL flag, their second straight.

- The Tigers down Chicago in six Series games. Tommy Bridges posts two complete victories for Detroit.

1936

Gehrig enjoys monster summer... Hubbell stretches win streak to 24... Cobb leads first inductees into Hall

- The Yankees' Lou Gehrig is AL MVP. Gehrig leads the majors in homers (49), runs (167), OBP (.478), SA (.696), walks (130), and runs produced (270). He also hits 14 homers vs. Cleveland, setting an ML record versus one club in a season.

- The Giants' Carl Hubbell wins his second NL MVP Award. He wins an all-time ML-record 24 straight games over a two-year period. His 26 wins top the majors.

- Chicago's Luke Appling wins the AL bat crown with a .388 BA, highest in the 20th century by an ML shortstop.

- Pittsburgh's Paul Waner wins his last NL bat crown (.373).

- Cleveland's Hal Trosky leads the ML in total bases (405) and RBI (162).

- The Hall of Fame is created. In the first vote for enshrinement, the leading vote-getter is Ty Cobb. Babe Ruth, Honus Wagner, Christy Mathewson, and Walter Johnson join Cobb as the first Hall electees.

- Ducky Medwick cracks an all-time NL-record 64 doubles. Medwick paces the NL in total bases (367), RBI (138), hits (223), and runs produced (235).

- On August 23, 17-year-old Indian Bob Feller sets a new AL record (since broken) when he fans 17 batters in a game.

> **"I can remember a reporter asking for a quote, and I didn't know what a quote was. I thought it was some kind of soft drink."**
>
> —*Yankee Joe DiMaggio, reflecting on his rookie season*

- Pirate Woody Jensen's 696 at-bats are the most by anyone on a 154-game schedule.

- The Yankees' Joe DiMaggio scores 132 runs, setting an AL rookie record. He breaks into the bigs on May 3 with a triple and two singles at St. Louis.

- Chuck Klein, back with the Phils, hits four homers in a 10-inning game on July 10.

- The NL wins the All-Star Game for the first time, 4-3 at Braves Field.

- The Yankees collect an ML-record 2,703 total bases. The team produces an ML-record 995 RBI.

- Detroit's Tommy Bridges tops the AL with 23 wins and 175 Ks.

- On May 24, Yankee Tony Lazzeri becomes the first major-leaguer to hit two grand slams in a game. He drives in an AL-record 11 runs.

- The Yankees win the AL by a record 19½ games over defending champion Detroit. New York finishes 102-51. Six regulars bat .300 or better, and five Yankees drive in at least 100 runs.

- The Giants set up the first "Subway Series" since 1923 by overtaking the Cubs and Cardinals in the NL. New York does it by winning 15 consecutive games during one stretch, sparked by Hubbell's personal win string.

- The Yankees take their first of four straight Series championships, turning back the Giants in six. Two of their four wins over the Giants come by scores of 18-4 (Game 2) and 13-4 (Game 6). Each of those two games feature 17 Yankee base hits.

Medwick wears the Triple Crown... Beaning ends career of Cochrane... Yankee express rumbles on

- The Cardinals' Ducky Medwick is named NL MVP. In the All-Star Game, he is the first player to collect four hits. Medwick wins the NL's last Triple Crown, batting .374 with 31 homers and 154 RBI. He also leads the NL in runs (111), hits (237), doubles (56), SA (.641), runs produced (234), and total bases (406).

- The Tigers' Charlie Gehringer is the AL MVP. He also wins the AL bat title at .371.

- The Giants' Carl Hubbell again leads the majors in wins with 22. Hubbell tops the NL in winning pct. (.733) and Ks (159).

- New York's Lou Gehrig is runner-up for the AL bat crown (.351), hitting .300 for the last time.

- Pirate Gus Suhr's NL-record streak of 822 consecutive games ends (record since broken).

- Detroit's Rudy York sets ML records with 18 homers and 49 RBI in a month (August).

- On May 25, Detroit's Mickey Cochrane is beaned by Yankee Bump Hadley, ending Cochrane's playing career.

- The AL decides that fans can keep balls hit into the stands after a federal court awards $7,500 to David Levy, whose skull was fractured in a scrap with Yankee Stadium ushers when he had tried to retrieve a foul ball hit by Gehrig.

- The Braves have two rookie 20-game winners, Lou Fette and Jim Turner; both are over age 30. Turner leads the NL in ERA (2.38) and ties for the lead in shutouts (five).

- Cleveland's Johnny Allen tops the AL with a loop-record .938 winning pct. Allen wins his first 15 starts of the season, then loses on the season's closing day.

At 34, Detroit's Charlie Gehringer sets an AL record for the oldest player to win his first batting title.

- Pirate pitcher Red Lucas leads the NL in pinch hits for the fourth time.

- New York's Mel Ott ties Medwick for the NL homer crown (31) and leads in walks (102).

- The Yankees' Joe DiMaggio tops the AL in runs (151) and total bases (418).

- Detroit's Hank Greenberg tops the AL in runs produced (280).

- Beau Bell of the Browns leads the AL in hits (218) and doubles (51).

- New York's Lefty Gomez tops the AL in wins (21), shutouts (six), Ks (194), and ERA (2.33).

Joe Medwick

- Cleveland's Bob Feller, in his first full season, Ks 150 batters in 149 innings.

- The Yankees have three men with 130-plus RBI—DiMaggio (167), Gehrig (159), and Bill Dickey (133).

- There is no stopping the Yankees, who win 102 games for the second straight year and roll to a 13-game margin over Detroit for the AL flag. The team scores the most runs in the AL (979) while allowing the fewest (671).

> **"The secret to my success was clean living and a fast-moving outfield."**
>
> —*Yankee Lefty Gomez*

- The Giants also repeat, edging the high-scoring Cubs by three games in the NL. Ott's 95 RBI and the sterling defense of shortstop Dick Bartell pave the way for the New Yorkers.

- A second consecutive "Subway Series" goes to the Yanks. Hubbell's win in Game 4 keeps the Giants from being swept, but the Yankees win the next one 4-2. Gomez, one of the worst hitting pitchers in baseball, drives in the winning run on a fifth-inning single. He finishes the Series 2-0 with a 1.50 ERA.

Gehrig clears 'em all for 23rd, final time... Vander Meer fires back-to-back no-hitters... Feller fans 18

- Boston's Jimmie Foxx is named AL MVP. Foxx wins the AL bat crown (.349) and also leads in RBI (175), SA (.704), runs produced (264), and total bases (398).

- Cincinnati's Ernie Lombardi is the NL MVP. Lombardi is the first catcher to win a consensus bat title (.348). (Bubbles Hargrave in 1926 had fewer than 400 at-bats.)

- Detroit's Hank Greenberg slugs 58 homers to lead the AL. Greenberg hits a record 39 homers at home. He also leads the AL in runs (144) and ties for the lead in walks (119).

- Cub Bill Lee leads the majors with 22 wins. Lee tops the majors in shutouts (nine) and ERA (2.66).

- Cardinal Frenchy Bordagaray sets an NL record with a .465 BA as a pinch hitter and gets 20 pinch hits.

- The Yankees' Lou Gehrig has 100 or more RBI for the 13th consecutive season, setting an ML record. Gehrig hits the last of his all-time ML-record 23 grand slams.

- Cincinnati's Johnny Vander Meer no-hits Boston on June 11. Vander Meer becomes the only pitcher in ML history to throw back-to-back no-hitters, as he blanks the Dodgers on June 15.

- The Phils move to Shibe Park on July 4 after 51 years in the Baker Bowl.

Jimmie Foxx

- On October 2, Bob Feller fans an ML-record 18 batters (since broken). Feller's 240 Ks top the majors; NL K leader Clay Bryant of Chicago has just 135.

- Red Sox Pinky Higgins sets an ML record with 12 hits in 12 consecutive at-bats.

- In April, the Cardinals send Dizzy Dean to the Cubs for three players and $185,000.

- George McQuinn of the Browns hits safely in 34 consecutive games.

- Mace Brown of Pittsburgh sets a major-league record by winning 15 games in relief.

- The Giants, Dodgers, and Yankees allow their home games to be broadcast on a regular basis.

- The Yanks' 9½-game margin of victory in the AL is their slimmest in the last three years, but does not constitute a tight race. The Bronx Bombers score a league-high 966 runs. Their 3.91 ERA is the only sub-4.00 mark in the AL.

- New York's Red Ruffing tops the AL in wins (21) and winning pct. (.750).

- Pitcher Red Lucas retires with 114 career pinch hits, an ML record to this juncture.

- New York's Mel Ott tops the NL in homers (36) and runs (116).

- St. Louis's Ducky Medwick paces the NL in doubles (47), RBI (122), and runs produced (201).

- Cardinal Johnny Mize leads the NL in slugging (.614), triples (16), and total bases (326).

Red Sox Doc Cramer sets an AL mark by going homerless for the season in 658 at-bats.

- The Cubs win their first NL pennant since 1935 in a race that turns Chicago's way in a late-season win over Pittsburgh. With darkness setting in, Cubs catcher Gabby Hartnett breaks a 5-5, ninth-inning tie with what comes to be known as the "homer in the gloaming." Chicago wins 20 of its last 23 games.

- The Yankees overpower the Cubs in one of the most lopsided Series to date. The four-game sweep features a run differential of 22-9.

Gehrig delivers emotional farewell speech... Rookie Williams bursts onto scene... Yankees make it four in a row

- The Yankees' Joe DiMaggio is named AL MVP. DiMaggio leads the majors with a .381 BA. He is the last righty to top .380 in a season.

- Cincinnati's Bucky Walters cops the NL MVP Award. Walters leads the majors with 27 wins; teammate Paul Derringer wins 25. Walters also tops the ML in innings (319) and ERA (2.29).

- Lou Gehrig's string of 2,130 consecutive games played ends on May 2. Gehrig gives his famous farewell address at Yankee Stadium after he learns he has amyotrophic lateral sclerosis. He is the first MLer to have his uniform number retired.

- On August 26, a major-league game is televised for the first time—Reds vs. Dodgers at Ebbets Field.

- On May 16, the first AL night game is played—Indians versus A's at Shibe Park.

- The Hall of Fame is officially dedicated and opens on June 12. Gehrig is voted into the Hall by a special ballot.

- Lefty Grove of the Red Sox wins the last of his ML-record nine ERA crowns (2.54).

- Boston rookie Ted Williams leads the majors in RBI with 145—a record for an ML rookie. Williams tops the majors in runs produced with 245.

- The use of netting in gloves is outlawed. Only leather webbing is allowed.

- In August, the Yankees' Red Rolfe scores at least one run in 18 consecutive games. Rolfe tops the AL in runs (139), hits (213), and doubles (46).

- Red Sox Jim Tabor hits two grand slams in a game on July 4.

- The sacrifice fly rule is reinstated.

- Boston's Jimmie Foxx leads the AL in homers (35) and slugging (.694).

- The Cardinals' Johnny Mize paces the NL in homers (28), BA (.349), SA (.626), and total bases (353).

- Johnny Murphy of the Yankees leads the majors with 19 saves, appearing in 38 games.

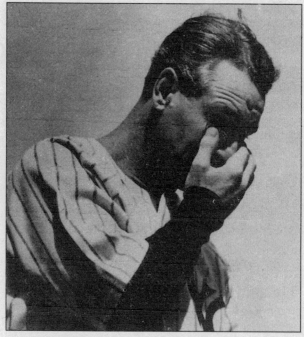

Lou Gehrig

- Cleveland's Bob Feller leads the AL in wins (24), innings (297), and Ks (246). At age 18, he becomes the youngest modern-era pitcher to win 20 games in a season.

- Red Frank McCormick again leads the NL in hits (209). He also leads in RBI (128) and runs produced (209).

- The Browns flail to a 43-111 record, finishing a record 64½ games out of first place in the AL. Their home success rate is a record-low 18-59.

- Cincinnati manager Bill McKechnie becomes the first ML skipper to win pennants with three different teams.

- The Reds, two years after finishing in last place, win the NL pennant by 4½ games over St. Louis.

> **"Today, I consider myself the luckiest man on the face of the earth."**
>
> —*Lou Gehrig, during his tearful farewell speech of July 4*

- Joe McCarthy's Yankees leave the rest of the AL in their wake, amassing a 17-game margin for their fourth flag in a row. Their 106-45 record is a combination of the most potent lineup and stingiest pitching staff in the league.

- Charlie Keller bats .438 with three homers and six RBI in the Yankees' four-game sweep of the Reds for their record fourth straight World Series title. It caps a four-year stretch in which New York wins 16 of 19 Series games.

1940

Feller wastes no time allowing no hits... Reds maintain MVP streak, win Series... Greenberg serves Tigers, then country

- Frank McCormick is named NL MVP—the third different Red in as many years to win the award. McCormick ties an NL record when he leads the loop in hits (191) for the third consecutive season.

- Detroit's Hank Greenberg is voted AL MVP. Greenberg tops the AL in homers (41) and tops the majors in RBI (150), doubles (50), runs produced (238), SA (.670), and total bases (384). After the season, Greenberg becomes the first MLer to enlist in the armed services in preparation for WWII.

- Johnny Mize of the Cardinals tops the NL in RBI (137), homers (43), SA (.636), and total bases (368).

- The Indians are nicknamed "The Crybabies" when they go to club owner Alva Bradley and demand he fire manager Ossie Vitt.

- Cleveland's Bob Feller pitches an Opening Day no-hitter on April 16 versus Chicago. Feller's 27 wins lead the majors. He also tops the AL in innings (320), complete games (31), and ERA (2.61). His 261 Ks are the most by any pitcher in the majors since 1924.

- Yankee Joe DiMaggio takes his second consecutive AL bat crown (.352).

- Pittsburgh's Debs Garms wins the NL bat title (.355).

- The Reds win 41 one-run games to set an ML record.

- Willis Hudlin is the first player since 1904 to play with four different teams in the same year.

- The sacrifice fly rule is again abolished.

- Boston's Ted Williams leads the AL in runs (134) and OBP (.442) and is third in batting (.344).

- Cincy's Bucky Walters leads the NL in complete games (29), innings (305), and ERA (2.48).

- Detroit's Rudy York, second in the AL in RBI with 134, combines with teammate Greenberg for 284 runs batted in.

- Reds catcher Willard Hershberger commits suicide.

For the first time since the Hall of Fame opens for inductions, no one is elected for the Cooperstown shrine.

- Cleveland shortstop Lou Boudreau has 101 RBI and tops AL shortstops in assists, DPs, and FA.

- The Phillies and A's both lose 100 games and finish in last place.

- The Cubs finish below .500 for the first time in 15 years.

- The Tigers put a temporary halt to the Yankee dynasty, preventing New York from winning a fifth straight AL pennant. First-year manager Del Baker earns much of the credit for his decision to move Greenberg to left field, thus opening a position at first base for York. The Indians finish one game back; the Yankees two.

- The Reds run away from the NL for their second straight flag, winning by a league-record 12 games over the Dodgers. Cincinnati wins 100 regular-season games.

- Forty-year-old Reds catcher Jimmie Wilson, playing for injured Ernie Lombardi, is the unlikely World Series hero, hitting .353 as Cincinnati tops the Tigers in seven games. It is the first Series win for the NL since 1934.

- Game 7 turns out to be one of the more exciting Series finales in history. The Reds' Paul Derringer holds the Tigers to one run on seven hits for a complete-game, 2-1 victory. He gets his only lead in the seventh inning with the help of doubles by Frank McCormick and Jimmy Ripple.

- The Reds' Derringer and Bucky Walters each collect two complete-game wins in the Series.

Bob Feller

DiMaggio hits in 56 straight games... Williams tops .400 with classy twin-bill finish... Gehrig dies at age 37

- Brooklyn's Dolph Camilli is the NL MVP. Camilli leads the NL in homers (34) and RBI (120).

- New York's Joe DiMaggio wins the AL MVP Award. DiMaggio strings together an ML-record 56-game hitting streak. He leads the majors in RBI (125) and total bases (348).

- Boston's Ted Williams, batting .39955 on the last day of the season, closes with a 6-for-8 performance in a doubleheader to finish at .406. With this effort, he becomes the last ML player to hit .400 or more. He leads the AL in runs (135), homers (37), OBP (.551), runs produced (218), walks (145), and SA (.735). In the All-Star Game, he hits a three-run homer with two out in the bottom of the ninth to give the AL a 7-5 win at Detroit.

- On March 8, Hugh Mulcahy of the Phils becomes the first MLer to be drafted in WWII.

Joe DiMaggio

- Brooklyn's Pete Reiser, age 22, becomes the youngest in history to win the NL bat crown (.343). Reiser paces the NL in runs (117), doubles (39), triples (17), runs produced (179), SA (.558), and total bases (299).

- Lou Gehrig dies on June 2 at age 37.

- The Phils lose a franchise-record 111 games.

- The Tigers give $52,000 to Dick Wakefield, who becomes the first of what will soon become a flurry of big-bucks bonus babies.

- Cleveland's Bob Feller tops the majors in wins with 25. Feller's 343 innings pitched are the most in the ML since 1923. He tops the majors again with 260 Ks and also leads the AL in shutouts with six. At the end of the season, Feller enlists in the Navy.

"I'm tickled to death it's over."

—*Yankee Joe DiMaggio, after the streak came to an end*

- The Dodgers become the first team to wear plastic batting helmets after Reiser and Pee Wee Reese are beaned.

- Wes Ferrell leaves the game with an ML-record 38 homers by a pitcher.

- White Sox Taffy Wright collects at least one RBI in an all-time AL-record 13 straight games.

- Cincinnati's Elmer Riddle tops the NL in both winning pct. (.826) and ERA (2.24).

- Lefty Grove wins his 300th game, becoming the last to accomplish the feat until 1963.

- Jeff Heath of Cleveland becomes the first in AL history to hit at least 20 homers, 20 triples, and 20 doubles in a season.

- The Yankees return to the top in grand fashion, going 101-53 to outpace the Red Sox by a whopping 17 games. There are no 20-game winners on the pitching staff, but the lineup is among the most potent ever assembled.

- The NL also has a 100-game winner in the Dodgers. Leo Durocher's squad posts a 100-54 mark, 2½ games better than the Cardinals.

- The World Series pits the Bronx against Brooklyn for the first time in what will become a regular fall rivalry.

- The Yankees win the Series in five games, with the turning point coming in Game 4. With a 4-3 lead in the ninth inning, the Dodgers' Hugh Casey strikes out Tommy Henrich for what should be the game's final out. But the ball gets past catcher Mickey Owen, Henrich reaches first base, and the Yanks go on to win 7-4.

1942

Triple Crown, not MVP, goes to Williams... Boudreau a skipper at 24... Ott wins his final home run title

- Mort Cooper of the Cards is the NL MVP. He tops the NL in wins (22), ERA (1.77), and shutouts (10).

- Joe Gordon of the Yanks is named AL MVP. Gordon leads the league in errors, strikeouts, and double plays grounded into, though he hits .322 with 103 RBI.

- Boston's Ted Williams wins the Triple Crown (.356 BA, 36 homers, 137 RBI) but once again loses out on the MVP vote. Williams also leads the AL in runs (141), walks (145), runs produced (242), total bases (338), OBP (.499), and SA (.648).

- The Phils finish last for the fifth consecutive year, setting an NL record.

- The Dodgers' 104 wins tie an ML record for the most wins by an also-ran.

- Cleveland's Lou Boudreau, age 24, is the youngest manager to begin the season at the helm of an ML team.

- The Cardinals' Johnny Beazley wins 21 games as a rookie, enters the armed services, and will never again be an effective pitcher.

- Boston's Tex Hughson tops the AL in wins (22) and innings (281) and ties for the lead in Ks (113) and complete games (22).

- New York's Mel Ott wins his last NL home run crown (30).

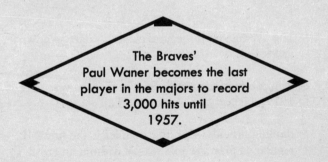

The Braves' Paul Waner becomes the last player in the majors to record 3,000 hits until 1957.

- Red Sox rookie Johnny Pesky hits .331 and tops the majors with 205 hits.

- White Sox Ted Lyons goes 14-6 as he makes just 20 mound appearances, all of them complete games.

Ted Williams

- The average major-league player's salary is down to $6,400.

- Run production in both leagues is the lowest since 1919, the last year of the dead-ball era.

- Phillie outfielder Danny Litwhiler is the first ML regular to play a whole season without an error.

- On August 14, the Yankees set an ML record with seven DPs versus the A's.

- On May 13, Brave Jim Tobin becomes the only pitcher in the 20th century to hit three homers in a game.

- Gordon and shortstop Phil Rizzuto set an AL keystone record (since broken) when they combine for 235 DPs.

- St. Louis's Enos Slaughter leads the NL in hits (188), triples (17), total bases (292), and runs produced (185).

- The Yankees repeat their AL pennant, posting a 103-51 record to come in nine games ahead of second-place Boston. Joe DiMaggio finishes second to Williams in runs (123) and RBI (114) while batting .305. Pitchers Tiny Bonham, Spud Chandler, and Hank Borowy are among the top five in ERA.

- The Cardinals, who trailed Brooklyn by 10 games in August, rally past the Dodgers to win the NL pennant. The Cards finished the season on a 43-8 tear under the leadership of Branch Rickey, winding up with a 106-48 mark.

- The Cardinals are the first team since 1926 to beat the Yankees in a World Series, winning in five games. Red Ruffing of the Yanks wins the opener, becoming the first pitcher to claim seven career Series games. The Cards take the next four, with Beazley going 2-0 with a 2.50 ERA.

- After the season, Rickey resigns as vice-president of a Cardinal team for which he built a model farm system. He replaces Larry MacPhail as president of the Dodgers.

Baseball tries, scraps balata ball... White Sox double up 44 times... Yankees find way back to summit

- Yankee pitcher Spud Chandler accepts the AL MVP Award. He leads the league in ERA (1.64) and winning pct. (.833) and ties in wins (20), complete games (20), and shutouts (five).

- Stan Musial is named NL MVP, beating out Cardinal teammate Walker Cooper. Musial wins his first NL bat crown (.357). He also leads the NL in OBP (.425), SA (.562), hits (220), doubles (48), triples (20), and total bases (347).

- Chicago's Luke Appling becomes the lone AL shortstop to win two bat crowns (.328).

- Detroit's Rudy York tops the AL in homers (34), RBI (118), runs produced (174), SA (.527), and total bases (301).

- Chicago's Bill Nicholson leads the NL in homers (29) and RBI (128).

- ML teams conduct spring training in northern sectors due to WWII travel restrictions.

- The Browns add to their ongoing ML record when they complete their 42nd season without having won a pennant.

- Washington's George Case wins his fifth consecutive AL theft crown (61).

- To save on rubber, a new balata baseball is introduced. There are no homers in the first 11 games of the season, and the new ball is shelved.

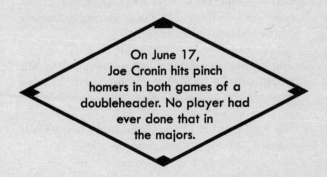

On June 17, Joe Cronin hits pinch homers in both games of a doubleheader. No player had ever done that in the majors.

- New York's Mel Ott is second in the NL with 18 homers. All 18 are hit in his home park.

- The White Sox play an ML-record 44 doubleheaders.

- The bankrupt Phils franchise is sold to the NL. William Cox becomes owner. Later, Commissioner Kenesaw Mountain Landis bans Cox for life for betting on his own team.

- The A's lose an AL-record (since broken) 20 straight games.

- In September, Philly's Carl Scheib, age 16, becomes the youngest player ever to appear in an AL game.

- The AL wins the first All-Star Game played at night, 5-3 at Shibe Park.

- Detroit rookie Dick Wakefield tops the AL in hits (200) and doubles (38) and is second in batting (.316) and total bases (275).

- The Giants' Ace Adams sets a new modern ML record with 70 mound appearances. His 11 relief wins are also a new standard.

- The total number of home runs in the majors falls below 1,000 for the first time since 1927.

- In April, Braves manager Casey Stengel is hit by a Boston taxi and lost to the team for 45 games.

- Their seventh AL pennant in eight years comes easily for the Yanks, by 13½ games over the Senators. A 36-year-old Bill Dickey is New York's leading hitter, with a .351 average.

- The Cardinals also repeat in the NL, using their deep farm system and rich talent to overcome losses due to the war effort. Players such as Lou Klein, Alpha Brazle, and Harry Brecheen step in for Enos Slaughter, Terry Moore, Johnny Beazley, and Howie Pollet. The Reds are a distant second, 18 games behind.

- The Yankees turn the tables on the Cards, winning the Series in five games. Chandler posts two wins and an ERA of 0.50. Walker Cooper registers the only St. Louis win after hearing that his father has died earlier in the day.

Spud Chandler

Browns end their record slump with only pennant... Cardinals kings of St. Louis... Gedeon killed in action

- Cardinal shortstop Marty Marion is named the NL MVP.

- Detroit's Hal Newhouser wins the AL MVP Award. Newhouser wins 29 games for the second-place Tigers, most since 1931 by an ML lefty.

- Dizzy Trout wins 27 for the Tigers to give the club a post-dead ball tandem record of 56 wins from two pitchers. Trout is second in the AL MVP voting. This is the first time two pitchers from the same team have finished one-two.

- Brooklyn's Dixie Walker tops the NL in batting at .357.

- Cleveland's Lou Boudreau wins the AL bat title at .327. Boudreau is involved in 134 DPs, an all-time major-league record for shortstops in a 154-game season.

- Cub Bill Nicholson tops the majors in homers with 33 and RBI with 122. Nicholson leads the NL in runs (116), runs produced (205), and total bases (317).

- AL homer leader Nick Etten of the Yankees belts just 22.

- Yankee Snuffy Stirnweiss, a .219 hitter in 1943, leads the majors with 205 hits. Stirnweiss tops the AL in runs (125) and steals (55) and ties for the lead in triples (16).

- Elmer Gedeon becomes the first former major-leaguer to be killed in action in WWII.

- On June 10, the Reds use 15-year-old pitcher Joe Nuxhall, the youngest player in the 20th century.

- Cincinnati's Ray Mueller sets an NL record when he participates in 217 consecutive games as a catcher.

- At the end of August, the Cards have a 91-30 mark, but they go only 14-19 the rest of the way. The Redbirds lead the majors in batting (.275), runs (772), homers (100), fielding (.982), and ERA (2.67).

- On April 27 versus the Dodgers, Jim Tobin of the Braves becomes the first pitcher to hit a homer while tossing a no-hitter.

Hal Newhouser

- On August 10, Red Barrett of the Braves throws just 58 pitches in a CG shutout of the Reds.

- St. Louis's Stan Musial tops the NL in doubles (51) and SA (.549) and ties for the lead in hits (197).

- The drought is over for the St. Louis Browns, who win their first nine games of the season and hold on to edge Detroit by a single game for the AL pennant. The Browns, a modest 89-65, end their 42-year string of futility by beating the Yankees five times in the season's final week.

- It's an All-Mound City World Series, as the Cardinals grab their third consecutive NL flag. By winning 105 games, they become the first team in NL history to win 100 or more games in three successive years.

> Bill Voiselle works 313 innings for the Giants, making him the last rookie pitcher to go 300-plus innings in a major-league season.

- The Cardinals defeat the Browns in six games, despite a .438 batting average and five RBI by the Browns' George McQuinn. Poor defense hurts the NL champs, including a combined six errors from the shortstop and second base positions. Cardinal pitchers notch a 1.96 ERA.

- One month after the Series, 78-year-old commissioner Kenesaw Mountain Landis dies. His 35-year tenure atop baseball is remembered for his tough stance against gambling-related corruption, and his surprising sympathy for the players in disputes with the owners.

1945

*All-Star Game a casualty of war...
Chandler selected game's new commish
... Tigers foil Cubs in seven-game Series*

- Detroit's Hal Newhouser wins his second straight AL MVP Award. Newhouser tops the majors with 25 wins, a .735 winning pct., a 1.81 ERA, 212 Ks, eight shutouts, and 29 complete games.

- Chicago's Phil Cavarretta is named the NL MVP.

- Boston's Tommy Holmes hits in 37 consecutive games—a modern NL record. Holmes is the only player ever to lead the league in homers (28) and fewest batter Ks (nine). He tops the NL in hits (224), doubles (47), total bases (367), and SA (.577).

- One-armed outfielder Pete Gray plays the full season for the Browns, hitting .218.

- On August 20, Dodgers shortstop Tommy Brown, age 17, becomes the youngest player in ML history to homer.

- Brooklyn's Dixie Walker tops the majors with 124 RBI and 218 runs produced.

- Yankee Snuffy Stirnweiss tops the AL in BA at just .309. Stirnweiss leads the AL in runs (107), SA (.476), steals (33), hits (195), triples (22), and total bases (301).

- Brooklyn's Branch Rickey signs Jackie Robinson to a contract.

- Happy Chandler is named the new commissioner of baseball.

- The All-Star Game is not held due to the war—its only cancellation in history.

> **"For the Washington Senators, the worst time of the year is the baseball season."**
>
> —Roger Kahn

- Philly's Andy Karl pitches 167 innings in relief to set an NL record that will last until 1974.

- Brooklyn's Eddie Stanky sets a new NL record for walks with 148.

- Bert Shepard, a one-legged pitcher, appears in a game for Washington.

- The Senators hit only one home run in their home park—and that's an inside-the-park homer by Joe Kuhel.

- On July 21, the Tigers and A's play to a 1-1 tie in 24 innings. Les Mueller pitches 19⅔ innings for the Tigers.

- The Cubs sweep an all-time ML-record 20 doubleheaders to break their own year-old mark.

- Cleveland plays only 147 games, the fewest in history by a team on a 154-game schedule.

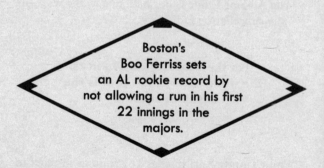

Boston's Boo Ferriss sets an AL rookie record by not allowing a run in his first 22 innings in the majors.

- A rule is adopted that says a player must have a minimum of 400 at-bats to qualify for a hitting title.

- The Cards lose Stan Musial and Walker Cooper to the armed services prior to the season and finish three games in back of the Cubs without them.

- The Cubs' success features the hitting of Cavarretta and Stan Hack, but it is pitching that's most responsible. Ray Prim, Claude Passeau, and Hank Wyse finish first, second, and fifth in the NL in ERA.

- Though Newhouser wins the MVP, it's the return of Greenberg from the war that ignites the Tigers to the AL flag in a close race with the Yankees, Senators, and Browns. Greenberg hits 13 homers in 270 at-bats, including one in his first game back and a grand slam on the season's final day.

- Greenberg continues his heroic play in the Series, a seven-game classic. His .304 hitting, two home runs, and seven RBI help the Tigers outlast the Cubs. His surprise sacrifice bunt is a key to Detroit's five-run first inning in its 9-3 Game 7 win.

- Tavern owner Billy Sianis brings his goat to a Series game at Wrigley Field and is denied admission. He thus puts a hex on the team, which some fans feel is responsible for the Cubs' failures over the rest of the century.

1946

Williams treats home crowd to two All-Star jacks... Yanks draw two million ...Brecheen picks up three Series wins

- Boston's Ted Williams is selected AL MVP. Williams tops the loop in SA (.667), total bases (343), runs (142), runs produced (227), OBP (.497), and walks (156).

- St. Louis's Stan Musial is named NL MVP. Musial paces the majors in batting (.365), total bases (366), hits (228), and triples (20). He tops the NL in runs (124), doubles (50), and SA (.587).

- The AL wins the most one-sided All-Star Game of the century, 12-0 at Fenway, as Williams belts two four-baggers.

- Cleveland's Bob Feller fans 348 in his first full year back from the Navy.

- Feller and Detroit's Hal Newhouser tie for the ML lead with 26 wins. Newhouser tops the majors in ERA (1.94) and is second in the AL MVP vote.

- Feller's 36 complete games are the most by a pitcher in the majors since the dead-ball era.

- Washington's Mickey Vernon leads the AL in batting at .353.

- Pittsburgh's Ralph Kiner is the first rookie to lead the NL in homers (23).

- Detroit's Hank Greenberg leads the majors with 44 homers and the AL with 127 RBI.

> **"When you win, you eat better, sleep better, and your beer tastes better. And your wife looks like Gina Lollobrigida."**
>
> —*Red Sox Johnny Pesky*

- Jackie Robinson becomes the first African-American to play a full season in organized baseball in the 20th century.

- The Mexican League lures several ML stars by offering them more money than the majors are paying.

- Buddy Rosar of the A's becomes the first regular catcher to sport a 1.000 fielding average for an entire season.

- The Yankees become the first team in ML history to draw more than two million at home.

- A four-man group, including John Galbreath and Bing Crosby, buys the Pirates.

- The players form the American Baseball Guild in their fourth attempt to unionize. The Guild helps raise the minimum ML salary to $5,000.

- Bill Kennedy of Rocky Mount in the Coastal Plains League fans 456 hitters and posts a 28-3 record with a 1.03 ERA.

Enos Slaughter, scoring Series-winning run

- Brooklyn's Pete Reiser steals home seven times, setting an ML record. He breaks his ankle with two weeks left in the season, however, hampering the Dodgers' chances of winning the pennant.

- Cardinal Howie Pollet is the NL ERA king (2.10) and also tops the NL in wins (21).

- Joe Cronin of the Red Sox is the first to manage two different AL teams to flags. Boston's 104-50 record is 12 games better than Detroit's. Williams, Johnny Pesky, and Dom DiMaggio lead the Sox offensively.

- The Cardinals and Dodgers tie for first place in the NL, setting up the league's first playoff. The Cards, with 25 hits, win the best-of-three affair in two games to take the pennant.

- While St. Louis and Brooklyn are settling the NL pennant, the Red Sox play an exhibition game against a team of AL All-Stars, and Williams takes a Milton Haefner pitch off the elbow. He bats only .200 in the World Series.

- Harry Brecheen wins three World Series games for the Cards, who outlast Boston in seven games. Enos Slaughter scores from first base on Harry Walker's double in the bottom of the eighth inning of the finale, giving St. Louis a 4-3 triumph for the championship.

Robinson breaks color barrier... Williams secures another Triple Crown... DiMaggio, Yankees rule again

- New York's Joe DiMaggio wins the American League MVP Award by one vote over Boston's Ted Williams, 202 to 201.

- Williams again wins the Triple Crown, batting .343 with 32 homers and 114 RBI. He leads the AL in runs (125), total bases (335), runs produced (207), walks (162), OBP (.499), and slugging (.634).

- Detroit's Hank Greenberg, the reigning AL homer and RBI king, is sold prior to the 1947 season to Pittsburgh for $75,000.

- Bob Elliott wins the NL MVP Award—the first Brave to do so since 1914.

- Harry Walker of the Phils, sent to them by the Cards, becomes the first player traded in midseason to win the NL bat crown (.363).

Jackie Robinson

- The Yanks tie an AL record by winning 19 straight games.

- Brooklyn's Jackie Robinson, the first African American to play in the majors, wins the Baseball Writers Association of America's first Rookie of the Year Award after batting .297 and stealing 29 bases.

- Al Lopez retires holding the record for most games at catcher—1,918 (since broken).

- New York's Johnny Mize and Pittsburgh's Ralph Kiner again tie for the NL homer crown (51).

- Cincinnati's Ewell Blackwell no-hits the Braves on June 18 and pitches eight hitless innings in his next start. Blackwell wins 16 straight games, a Cincinnati club record. He leads the NL in wins (22), complete games (23), and Ks (193).

- The Giants hit 221 homers, an ML record.

- Brooklyn manager Leo Durocher is suspended for the season by Commissioner Happy Chandler for associating with gamblers.

> **"Robinson will not make the grade in the major leagues. He is a thousand-to-one shot at best. The Negro players simply don't have the brains or the skills."**
>
> —*Sportswriter Jimmy Powers*

- Larry Doby debuts with Cleveland on July 5 to break the color line in the AL.

- Boston's Warren Spahn tops the NL in ERA (2.33), innings (290), and shutouts (seven) and posts 21 wins.

- Spud Chandler retires holding the record for the highest career winning pct. (.717) of any ML pitcher with at least 100 career wins.

- Attendance everywhere is at an all-time high as the postwar baseball boom is in full swing.

- Dan Bankhead of the Dodgers is the first African American to pitch in the majors.

- Mize tops the NL in RBI (138), runs (137), and runs produced (224).

- A reunited Yankees team scores the most runs in the AL (794), allows the fewest (568), and wins the pennant by 12 games over Detroit.

- In the NL, the Dodgers follow the lead of Robinson, Pee Wee Reese, Dixie Walker, and Pete Reiser to the pennant. Burt Shotton, after taking over for the suspended Durocher, manages the team to 94 wins and a five-game margin over the Cardinals.

- Yankee Bill Bevens comes within one out of a no-hitter in Game 4 of the Series, but he loses the game on a two-run double by Cookie Lavagetto.

- In an exciting but erratically played fall classic, the Yankees survive in seven games. Spec Shea wins two games on the mound for New York with a 2.35 ERA.

- The Yankees fire general manager Larry MacPhail after the Series for brawling in public.

Boudreau gains glory as player, skipper... Paige breaks new ground on hill... Cancer claims the Babe

- Cleveland's Lou Boudreau is the AL MVP. He's the last player/manager to win the award and the last to win a World Series. Boudreau tops AL shortstops in FA for the eighth time to tie an ML record. He is the first shortstop in AL history to hit over .350 and drive in more than 100 runs in the same season.

- St. Louis's Stan Musial is named NL MVP. Musial's 429 total bases are the most by any ML player from 1933 through the end of the century. He misses the Triple Crown by a margin of just one home run.

- Al Dark of the Braves is named Rookie of the Year and is third in the NL MVP vote.

- Rookie Gene Bearden wins 20 games for Cleveland, tops the AL in ERA (2.43), and wins the pennant playoff game vs. the Red Sox.

- Pittsburgh's Ralph Kiner and New York's Johnny Mize again tie for the NL homer crown (40).

- Johnny Sain of the Braves leads the majors with 24 wins.

- Boston's Ted Williams tops the AL in BA (.369), SA (.615), and OBP (.497).

- The Negro National League disbands, as most of its top players have jumped to the majors.

- Cleveland owner Bill Veeck signs Satchel Paige. Paige is the first African American to pitch in the AL and the first to pitch in a World Series game.

- Babe Ruth dies of throat cancer on August 16.

- Pat Seerey of the White Sox hits four homers in an 11-inning game on July 18.

> Cleveland's Satchel Paige, who is at least 42 years old in his rookie season in the majors and possibly closer to 50, finishes with a 6-1 record and two shutouts to go with a 2.48 ERA.

- The A's win 84 games. It's their best season from 1933 through 1968.

- Cardinal Harry Brecheen tops the NL in winning pct. (.741), ERA (2.24), Ks (149), and shutouts (seven).

- Cleveland's Bob Lemon leads the AL in innings pitched (294), complete games (20), and shutouts (10).

- New York's Joe DiMaggio tops the AL in RBI (155), homers (39), and total bases (355).

- Boston's Dom DiMaggio sets an AL record (since broken) with 503 outfield putouts.

- The Braves win their first NL pennant since 1914. Sain dominates on the mound and Warren Spahn goes 15-12 with 16 complete games, but no other Brave pitcher wins more than 13 games. Boston fans adopt the cry, "Spahn and Sain and pray for rain."

- Cleveland tops the AL in BA (.282), homers (155), ERA (3.22), and FA (.982) but barely wins the flag. The Indians ruin a potential all-Boston World Series by defeating the Red Sox 8-3 in a one-game playoff at Fenway Park. Boudreau hits two homers and two singles.

- Boudreau completes his remarkable year by guiding the Indians to the Series title in six games, despite losing twice with Bob Feller on the mound. Lemon is 2-0 with a 1.65 ERA.

- Casey Stengel, skipper of the Oakland Oaks of the Pacific Coast League, is hired to manage the Yankees during the 1949 season.

Stan Musial

1949

*Williams just misses Triple Crown...
DiMaggio's salary jumps to six
figures...Stengel debuts with world title*

- Brooklyn's Jackie Robinson is selected NL MVP. Robinson tops the NL in hitting (.342) and stolen bases (37).

- Boston's Ted Williams is the AL MVP. Williams paces the AL in homers (43) and ties for the lead in RBI (159). He loses the Triple Crown when he finishes a fraction behind Detroit's George Kell in batting, as both hit .343. He also tops the AL in runs (150), doubles (39), total bases (368), SA (.650), OBP (.490), and walks (162). Williams is the last player of the century to produce 250 or more runs in a season.

- Mel Parnell of the Red Sox tops the majors with 25 wins.

- The AL wins a wild All-Star Game, 11-7 at Brooklyn. This marks the first appearance of African-American players in an All-Star Game.

- Pittsburgh's Ralph Kiner wins his fourth consecutive NL homer crown with 54, threatening the NL record. Kiner hits 25 homers on the road—an NL record. He also paces the NL in RBI (127), walks (117), and SA (.658).

- Boston's Vern Stephens ties Williams for the AL RBI lead with 159, an ML record for shortstops.

- Yankee Joe Page sets an ML record with 27 saves.

- Joe DiMaggio signs the first $100,000 contract in ML history.

> **"There is always some kid who may be seeing me for the first or last time. I owe him my best."**
>
> —Joe DiMaggio

- The A's perform an all-time ML-record 217 double plays.

- New York's Dave Koslo tops the NL in ERA (2.50) and is the first leader without a shutout.

- St. Louis's Stan Musial tops the NL in hits (207), doubles (41), total bases (382), and OBP (.438) and ties in triples (13).

- The Cards have only 17 stolen bases—an all-time record low for an NL team.

- Boston's Dom DiMaggio has a 34-game hitting streak.

- The Red Sox collect an ML-record 835 walks.

- Boston's Warren Spahn tops the NL in wins (21), innings (302), complete games (25), and Ks (151).

> Pittsburgh's Ralph Kiner's 54-home run season makes him the first National Leaguer in history to hit 50 or more homers in two separate seasons. He first did it in 1947.

- Cincinnati's Walker Cooper goes 6-for-7 with three home runs in a nine-inning game.

- Casey Stengel, the Yankees' rookie manager, overcomes several obstacles in guiding his team to the AL pennant. He does it despite losing DiMaggio for half the season with a heel injury and pneumonia, and several other players to assorted ailments. Platooning is a key.

- The Red Sox, for the second straight year, lose the AL flag by a single game by dropping the final two games of the season to New York.

- The Dodgers win a close race with St. Louis for the NL pennant. One game is the final margin. Brooklyn manager Burt Shotton turns to a young lineup that includes, for the first time, Duke Snider in center field.

- The Cardinals contribute to their own demise by losing four games in the final week.

- The Series starts with Brooklyn and New York trading 1-0 decisions. Then the Yankees rally for three runs in the ninth inning to win Game 3 by a 4-3 score, gaining the momentum they need to close out the Dodgers in five. During the final game at Ebbets Field, lights are turned on for the first time in a World Series.

1950

All-Star Game decided on 14th-inning blast...Sisler's homer lifts Phils on final day...Yanks sweep Series

- Yankee shortstop Phil Rizzuto is selected AL MVP.

- Phillie Jim Konstanty is the NL MVP, becoming the first reliever to win the award.

- St. Louis's Stan Musial tops the NL in hitting (.346) and slugging (.596). Musial hits in 30 consecutive games.

- Red Sox Billy Goodman wins the AL bat crown (.354)—the only player ever to win the hit title without having a regular position.

- The NL wins the All-Star Game 4-3 at Comiskey Park, as St. Louis's Red Schoendienst homers in the 14th to win it.

- On May 18 vs. Brooklyn, Cardinal third sacker Tommy Glaviano makes errors on three straight plays, blowing the game.

- Cleveland's Bob Lemon tops the majors with 23 wins.

- Brooklyn's Gil Hodges hits four homers in a game on August 31.

- Cleveland's Early Wynn tops the AL with a 3.20 ERA—the highest ERA in ML history by a leader.

- A's manager Connie Mack retires after 50 years at the helm. His 3,731 wins and 3,948 losses are all-time records. He steps down with nine pennants, five Series titles, and 17 last-place finishes on his managing ledger.

> **"My best pitch is anything the batter grounds, lines, or pops in the direction of (Phil) Rizzuto."**
>
> —*Yankee Vic Raschi*

- All Mexican League jumpers are reinstated by organized baseball for the 1950 season after a suit by Danny Gardella vs. Happy Chandler. Sal Maglie, one of the jumpers, wins 18 games for the Giants and tops the NL in winning pct. (.818).

- On September 10, New York's Joe DiMaggio becomes the first to hit three homers in a game in Washington's Griffith Stadium.

- On June 8, the Browns are beaten 29-4 by the Red Sox at Fenway Park—the most lopsided game in the 20th century.

- On April 18 at St. Louis, the Cards and Pirates play the first "Opening Night" game in ML history.

- TV provides baseball with an extra $2.3 million in new revenues in 1950.

- Brooklyn's Duke Snider tops the NL in hits (199) and total bases (343).

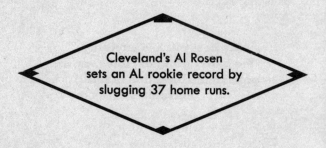

Cleveland's Al Rosen sets an AL rookie record by slugging 37 home runs.

- Yankee Vic Raschi sets an ML record (since broken) when he retires 32 batters in a row.

- A new balk rule is reinstated. On May 3, Raschi commits four balks in one game.

- Yankee Jackie Jensen plays in both the Rose Bowl and the World Series.

- Ted Williams breaks his elbow in the All-Star Game and is lost until September, dealing the Red Sox a huge blow in their quest for a pennant.

- The Phillies garner their first NL pennant since 1915, and they do it in dramatic fashion. Leading the Dodgers by one game entering the season finale at Ebbets Field, they turn back Brooklyn on a three-run, 10th-inning homer by Dick Sisler.

- The AL race is also decided by two games, with the 98-56 Yankees winning their second pennant in as many years under Stengel. Rizzuto, DiMaggio, Yogi Berra, and Hank Bauer all hit over .300. Raschi is the ace with 21 wins, and rookie Whitey Ford wins nine of his first 10 decisions after his recall from the minors.

- Philly's "Whiz Kids" lose by one run in each of the first three World Series games, then drop a 5-2 decision as the Yankees sweep. Jerry Coleman, who hits .286, wins the Babe Ruth Award as Series MVP. New York's Series ERA is 0.73.

1951

Thomson launches shot heard 'round the world... Kiner racks up sixth straight HR title... Joltin' Joe walks away

- Yankee catcher Yogi Berra claims the AL MVP Award.

- Dodger catcher Roy Campanella is named NL MVP.

- Giant teammates Sal Maglie and Larry Jansen tie for the ML lead in wins (23).

- St. Louis's Stan Musial tops the NL in batting (.355), runs (124), triples (12), total bases (355), and runs produced (200).

- Pittsburgh's Ralph Kiner wins his sixth consecutive NL homer crown (42). Kiner also leads the NL in walks (137), SA (.627), and OBP (.452).

- Ford Frick is named new commissioner after Happy Chandler's contract is not renewed by ML owners.

- Bill Veeck buys the Browns after selling the Indians. Veeck signs small person Eddie Gaedel, who appears in a game on August 19 as a pinch hitter and draws a walk.

- On July 1, Bob Feller becomes the first to throw three career no-hitters in the 20th century, as he blanks Detroit.

- Dodger Preacher Roe's .880 winning pct. is the highest in history by an NL 20-game winner.

- Boston's Warren Spahn leads the NL in complete games (26) and shutouts (seven) and ties in Ks (164).

- On September 14, Bob Nieman of the Browns becomes the only player in ML history to homer in his first two ML at-bats.

- Paul Lehner ties the AL record when he plays for four teams in the same year.

- On September 13, owing to rainouts, the Cards play the Giants at home in the afternoon and the Braves at home at night.

- Cleveland has three 20-game winners—Feller (22), Early Wynn (20), and Mike Garcia (20).

- Philadelphia's Gus Zernial tops the AL in home runs with 33.

- The Giants' Willie Mays is named NL Rookie of the Year after beginning the season in the minors.

- Braves rookie Chet Nichols tops the NL in ERA (2.88).

- Ferris Fain of the A's wins the AL batting title (.344).

- Chicago's Go-Go Sox lead the majors with 99 steals, one year after setting the AL record for fewest steals.

- Topps introduces its first baseball cards, in five sets.

- Mickey Mantle breaks into the Yankee lineup.

- The Giants win 16 games in a row in August, and 39 of their last 47 in the regular season, to pull into a first-place tie with Brooklyn. It sets up a best-of-three playoff for the NL flag.

- New York and Brooklyn split their first two playoff games, setting up the dramatic finale at the Polo Grounds. The Dodgers take a 4-1 lead into the bottom of the ninth, but two singles and a Whitey Lockman double make it 4-2 with Giant runners at second and third. Bobby Thomson then greets relief pitcher Ralph Branca by lining a three-run homer to left. Some call it the "shot heard 'round the world."

Bobby Thomson, NL playoff

- Casey Stengel steers the Yankees to a third pennant in as many years, using a lineup that features no .300 hitters. The Indians are second, five games back.

- A six-game World Series goes to the Yankees, despite wins by the Giants in two of the first three games. Monte Irvin's 11 hits for the Giants are one short of the Series record.

- Yankee Ed Lopat is the World Series pitching star with two complete-game wins and a 0.50 ERA.

- Joe DiMaggio announces his retirement at the conclusion of a Series in which he bats .261 with a homer and five RBI.

1952

Trucks tosses two Tiger no-nos...
Kiner wins another long-ball crown...
Yanks win Series on the road

- Cub Hank Sauer is named NL MVP. He leads the NL in RBI (121) and ties in homers (37).

- Robin Roberts wins 28 games for the Phils, most in the NL since 1935, but doesn't win MVP honors.

- Philly's Bobby Shantz wins the AL MVP Award. Shantz tops the loop with 24 wins.

- St. Louis's Stan Musial paces the majors with a .336 BA. Musial leads the NL in hits (194), slugging (.538), total bases (311), and doubles (42) and ties for the lead in runs (105).

- Philly's Ferris Fain wins his second consecutive AL bat crown (.327).

- Ted Williams leaves Boston to fight in the Korean War. The Red Sox tumble to sixth place.

- Pittsburgh's Ralph Kiner ties Sauer for the NL homer crown to give Kiner his seventh consecutive NL title.

- On April 23, Giant pitcher Hoyt Wilhelm homers in his first ML at-bat. He'll never homer again.

- For the first time in its history, the All-Star Game is curtailed by weather. The NL beats the AL 3-2 at Philadelphia's Shibe Park before rain stops play after five innings.

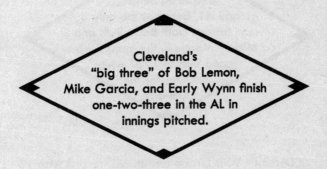

Cleveland's "big three" of Bob Lemon, Mike Garcia, and Early Wynn finish one-two-three in the AL in innings pitched.

- On May 21 in the first inning, 19 straight Dodgers reach base safely against the Reds.

- Virgil Trucks of Detroit no-hits Washington 1-0 on May 15. Trucks then no-hits the Yankees 1-0 on August 25. In another game against Washington, he allows a single to the first batter, then no-hits the Senators the rest of the way.

- The Pirates lose 112 games under new GM Branch Rickey, who was ousted by Dodgers owner Walter O'Malley the previous year.

- Tiger pitcher Fred Hutchinson is named team manager. He's the last pitcher to serve as player/manager.

> Red Sox pitcher Al Benton, age 41, becomes the only man to face both Babe Ruth and Mickey Mantle in the majors. He faced Ruth in 1937 while pitching for the Athletics.

- Detroit's Walt Dropo ties an ML record with 12 hits in 12 consecutive at-bats.

- On August 6, the Browns' Satchel Paige, at age 47, shuts out Detroit 1-0 in 12 innings.

- Pitcher Bill Thomas ends his career with 383 wins, the most ever in the minor leagues. He never gets a chance to pitch in the bigs.

- Cleveland's Larry Doby tops the AL in runs (104), homers (32), and SA (.541).

- Cleveland's Al Rosen leads the AL in RBI (105) and runs produced (178).

- Yankee Allie Reynolds paces the AL in ERA (2.06) and Ks (160).

- Brooklyn's Joe Black is the first African-American pitcher to win a World Series contest (Game 1). Black is the NL Rookie of the Year.

- With a two-game edge over the Indians, the Yankees win their fourth straight AL flag. It's a breakthrough season for Mickey Mantle, who bats .311 with 23 homers and 87 RBI. Yogi Berra clubs 30 homers and drives in 98.

- Jackie Robinson and Duke Snider top the .300 mark for a Dodger team that finishes 4½ games ahead of the Giants in the NL.

- The Dodgers win three of the first five Series games, and they need only one victory in the last two games at their own Ebbets Field to take the championship from the Yankees. Instead, New York wins 3-2 and 4-2 for their fourth consecutive world title.

*Boston's Braves pack bags for
Milwaukee... Campy sets new standard
for backstops... Make it a high five
for the Yanks*

- Cleveland's Al Rosen is named AL MVP. Rosen misses the Triple Crown when he loses the bat title by failing to beat out a ground ball in his final at-bat of the season. He hits .336 with 43 homers and 145 RBI. Rosen tops the AL in SA (.613), runs (115), total bases (367), and runs produced (217).

- Brooklyn's Roy Campanella wins his second NL MVP Award. Campanella's 41 homers set an ML record for catchers.

- Brooklyn's Carl Furillo takes the NL bat crown at .344.

- Milwaukee's Eddie Mathews leads the major leagues in home runs (47).

- Detroit rookie Harvey Kuenn tops the majors in hits (209). Kuenn is named AL Rookie of the Year.

- The Dodgers tie an ML record with six men scoring 100 runs or more. The team homers in an NL-record 24 straight games (since broken).

- Vic Janowicz of the Pirates becomes the first Heisman Trophy winner to play in the majors.

- The Braves move prior to the season to Milwaukee, creating the first ML franchise shift since 1903.

- Washington's Mickey Vernon wins his second AL bat title (.337).

Roy Campanella

- Phillie Robin Roberts tops the majors in complete games (33), Ks (198), and innings (347) and ties for the ML lead in wins (23).

- On May 6, the Browns' Bobo Holloman becomes the only pitcher in the 20th century to toss a no-hitter in his first ML start, as he blanks Philly.

> Carl Erskine of the Dodgers sets a World Series record by striking out 14 batters in the third game of the fall classic. Mickey Mantle fans four times in Brooklyn's 3-2 win.

- On June 18 in the seventh inning, the Red Sox score a 20th-century ML-record 17 runs. In that game, Red Sox Gene Stephens becomes the only player in modern ML history to get three hits in an inning.

- On May 25, Max Surkont of the Braves becomes the first in the 20th century to fan eight batters in a row in a game.

- Pittsburgh's O'Brien twins, Johnny and Eddie, each play 89 games for the Pirates.

- On April 17 in Washington, Mickey Mantle hits the longest measured home run in history—565 feet. Later in the game, Mantle bunts for a hit.

- Yankee Ed Lopat paces the AL in winning pct. (.800) and ERA (2.42).

- Milwaukee's Warren Spahn tops the NL in ERA (2.10) and ties Roberts for the lead in wins (23).

- The Yankees win nine of their first 11 games, take 18 in a row in May, and cruise to their fifth consecutive AL pennant. Casey Stengel becomes the first to manage a team to five straight flags.

- Brooklyn wins a club-record 105 games and becomes the first NL team to repeat since the 1944 Cardinals. The Braves finish second by 13 games. Dodger second baseman Junior Gilliam is named NL Rookie of the Year.

- Mantle homers power the Yanks to wins in Games 2 and 5 of the World Series. Billy Martin's 12th hit of the Series breaks a 3-all tie in the bottom of the ninth of the sixth and final game, as the Yankees post an all-time record fifth title in a row. Martin finishes with two homers, eight RBI, and a .500 average.

Another move: Browns head to Baltimore... Mays, Williams make dazzling returns... Giants pull off Series stunner

- Prior to the season, the Browns are sold and move to Baltimore, becoming the first AL franchise to move since 1903.

- New York's Willie Mays is named NL MVP. Mays tops the NL in batting (.345) and slugging (.667) after spending the previous two years in the armed services.

- Yankee catcher Yogi Berra is named AL MVP.

- On August 1 vs. the Dodgers, Milwaukee's Joe Adcock hits four homers and sets an ML record with 18 total bases.

- Players are no longer allowed to leave their gloves on the playing field while their team is batting.

- Boston's Ted Williams returns from Korean War duty and hits .345 for the season.

- Cleveland pitchers Mike Garcia, Bob Lemon, and Early Wynn rank one-three-four in ERA, Garcia leading at 2.64. Wynn and Lemon tie for the ML lead in wins with 23.

- Cleveland's Bobby Avila is awarded the AL batting title (.341) because Williams has fewer than 400 at-bats.

- Cleveland's Larry Doby tops the AL in homers (32) and RBI (126).

- The Giants' Johnny Antonelli paces the NL in winning pct. (.750) and ERA (2.30).

- On August 8 in the eighth inning, the Dodgers score 12 runs with two outs and the bases empty.

- Cards rookie Rip Repulski collects two or more hits in an ML-record 10 consecutive games.

- The sacrifice fly rule is reinstated once again.

- Cincy's Ted Kluszewski sets a 20th-century NL record when he scores at least one run in 17 consecutive games. Kluszewski tops the NL in homers (49) and RBI (141).

- On May 2, Stan Musial becomes the first to hit five homers in a doubleheader. Musial leads the NL in doubles (41) and runs produced (211) and ties in runs (120).

Willie Mays, World Series

- The AL wins the All-Star Game 11-9 in Cleveland, as hometown star Al Rosen hits two homers and knocks in five runs.

- After the season, the Yankees and Orioles make a record 18-player swap.

- Joe Bauman hits an organized-baseball record 72 home runs for Roswell of the Longhorn League.

- A step up from Bauman, Giant farmhand Bob Lennon hits 64 home runs for Nashville in the Southern Association. He will hit only one homer, with the Cubs three years later, in his brief career in the majors.

- In October, Marilyn Monroe files for divorce from Joe DiMaggio in California.

- After five straight world titles, the Yankees are dethroned in the AL pennant race by the Indians despite winning 103 games. That's because the Indians, appearing unbeatable, win a league-record 111.

- Leo Durocher's Giants beat the Dodgers by five games in the NL, with Mays setting the pace. Johnny Antonelli, with a 21-7 record, is New York's pitching ace.

- In one of the most shocking Series played to date, the Giants sweep the 111-win Indians in four games. Mays makes a spectacular, over-the-shoulder catch of Vic Wertz's 460-foot fly ball to center at the opener in the Polo Grounds.

- Dusty Rhodes bats .667 with two homers and seven RBI in the Giants' Series sweep. The Indians' pitching staff is bruised for a 4.84 ERA.

Young Kaline wastes little time... Mays, Mantle cop home run crowns... Dodgers end long string of Series misery

- New York's Yogi Berra is named AL MVP for the third time in five years.

- Brooklyn's Roy Campanella is the NL MVP for the second time in three years.

- Detroit's Al Kaline wins the AL bat title (.340) at age 20, making him the youngest bat crown winner in ML history. Kaline leads the AL in hits (200), total bases (321), and runs produced (196).

- Cleveland rookie Herb Score tops the AL in Ks with 245, setting an ML rookie record for Ks. Score is named AL Rookie of the Year.

- Phillie Richie Ashburn leads the NL in batting (.338).

- Philly's Robin Roberts again tops the NL in wins, as he earns 23.

- Dodger pitcher Don Newcombe cracks 42 hits and bats .359. Newcombe wins 20 games and tops the NL in winning pct. (.800).

- Cub rookie pitcher Toothpick Sam Jones sets a modern NL record with 185 walks. Jones no-hits the Pirates on May 12 after walking the bases full in the ninth and then fanning the side.

- Yankee Mickey Mantle wins his first AL homer crown (37). Mantle also leads the AL in OBP (.433), walks (113), and SA (.611) and ties in triples (11).

> For the first time in history, no AL pitcher is able to win as many as 20 games. Cleveland's Bob Lemon, New York's Whitey Ford, and Boston's Frank Sullivan each have 18.

- The most balanced Dodger team in years wins 20 of its first 22 games and never looks back under second-year manager Walter Alston. The Giants finish 13½ games behind in the NL flag chase.

- The Giants' Willie Mays leads the NL in homers (51), SA (.659), and total bases (382) and ties in triples (13).

- Brooklyn's Duke Snider leads the majors in runs (126), RBI (136), and runs produced (220).

- Elston Howard is the first African American to play for the Yankees, one of the last teams to break the color line.

- Billy Bruton of the Braves becomes the first in NL history to lead the league in steals in each of his first three seasons.

- Down 5-0 at one point, the NL rallies to win the All-Star Game 6-5 in 12 innings at Milwaukee.

- Cincinnati's Ted Kluszewski slams 47 home runs, giving him 136 homers and only 109 strikeouts from 1953 to '55.

- Calvin Griffith, adopted son of Clark, takes over as Senators president upon his father's death.

- Washington's Harmon Killebrew hits his first ML home run on June 24 at age 18.

- Ernie Banks of the Cubs hits five grand slams. With 44 home runs, he also becomes the first shortstop to hit 40 or more in a season.

- The Dodgers open the season with 10 straight wins.

- For the first time in history, no AL pitcher wins 20 games.

- Pirate Bob Friend leads the NL in ERA (2.84).

- The AL pennant goes to the Yankees for the sixth time in seven years. Cleveland winds up three games behind the Bronx Bombers.

- The World Series is a classic. New York wins the first two games, Brooklyn takes the next three, and Whitey Ford's four-hitter for the Yankees forces a seventh game at Yankee Stadium.

- Dodger pitcher Johnny Podres blanks the Yankees 2-0, clinching the first world title for Brooklyn. It is also the Yankees' first loss in a seven-game World Series since 1926.

Larsen picture perfect in Series milestone ... Put a Triple Crown on Mantle ... Mays off to the races

- Brooklyn's Don Newcombe wins the NL MVP Award. Newcombe also wins the first-ever Cy Young Award. (Only one is awarded each year until 1967.) Newcombe leads the majors in wins (27) and winning pct. (.794).

- Yankee Mickey Mantle is AL MVP. Mantle wins the Triple Crown, hitting .353 with 52 homers and 130 RBI. He is the first switch-hitter to lead a major league in batting since 1889. He leads the AL in runs (132), runs produced (210), SA (.705), and total bases (376).

- The Reds hit 221 homers to tie the ML record.

- In May, Dale Long of the Pirates hits home runs in an ML-record eight consecutive games.

- The Giants' Willie Mays tops the NL with 40 steals, most in the majors since 1944.

- The Reds' Frank Robinson clubs 38 homers to tie the ML rookie record. Robinson tops the NL in runs (122) and is named NL Rookie of the Year.

- Milwaukee's Hank Aaron wins the NL batting crown (.328). Aaron tops the NL in hits (200), total bases (340), doubles (34), and runs produced (172).

- The NL wins the All-Star Game 7-3.

- On September 21, the Yankees leave an ML-record 20 men on base in a nine-inning game vs. Boston.

- Jim Derrington of the White Sox, age 16, becomes the youngest pitcher in the 20th century to start a game.

- On May 26, three Reds pitchers throw a combined no-hitter vs. Milwaukee for nine innings but lose 2-1 in 11 innings.

- Brooklyn's Duke Snider tops the NL in homers (43), SA (.598), OBP (.402), and walks (99).

- Herb Score wins 20 for Cleveland and tops the majors in Ks (263) and AL in shutouts (five).

- Ernie Banks's record streak of 424 consecutive games played to start a career ends (record since broken).

- Cleveland once again has three 20-game winners, but finishes second to New York.

- White Sox Luis Aparicio tops the AL in thefts (21) and is named AL Rookie of the Year.

- New York's Whitey Ford leads the AL in winning pct. (.760) and ERA (2.47).

- Brooklyn hero Johnny Podres misses the season when he's inducted into the Navy.

"No. Why should I?"

—Don Larsen, when asked if he ever tired of talking about his World Series perfect game

- Connie Mack dies at age 93.

- The Yankees grab hold of first place in the AL on May 16 and never look back, winning by nine games over the Indians.

- The surprising Reds give the Dodgers and Braves a scare, but Brooklyn weathers Milwaukee by one game and Cincinnati ends up two games back.

- Don Larsen makes World Series history in one of the most memorable pitching gems of all time. The Yankees' fifth-game starter, using a no-windup style, sets down all 27 Dodgers for a perfect game and the only no-hitter in Series history.

⊗ The Dodgers come back to even the Series with a 1-0, 10-inning win in the next game, as Clem Labine hurls the extra-inning shutout. The finale is a 9-0 blowout in favor of the Yanks.

⊗ Yankee Yogi Berra tops all hitters in the World Series with a .360 BA and 10 RBI.

⊗ After the Series, Jackie Robinson retires after 10 seasons with Brooklyn.

Don Larsen

1957

*Aaron cops first home run crown...
Line drive ends Score's career... Giants,
Dodgers to switch coasts*

- The Braves' Hank Aaron is named NL MVP and wins his first NL homer crown (44). He also tops the NL in runs (118), RBI (132), total bases (369), and runs produced (206).

- Yankee Mickey Mantle repeats as AL MVP. He leads the league in runs (121) and walks (146).

- Boston's Ted Williams, at age 39, tops the AL with a .388 BA, highest in the majors since his own .406 in 1941. He also leads the AL in SA (.731) and OBP (.528). Williams reaches base in 16 consecutive plate appearances to set an all-time ML record.

- Milwaukee's Warren Spahn leads the majors with 21 wins and takes the Cy Young Award.

- St. Louis's Stan Musial wins his last NL bat crown (.351).

- The Senators steal 13 bases, fewest ever by an ML team.

- Cleveland's Herb Score is nearly killed when hit in the eye by a line drive. He'll never regain his overpowering fastball.

- The Giants and Dodgers both play their final games as New York-based teams. Citing inefficient parks and a lack of parking facilities, the owners of both teams take their clubs to California after the season.

> Duke Snider of the Dodgers becomes the first player ever to hit 40 or more homers in a season yet drive in less than 100 runs. His totals are 40 home runs and 92 RBI.

- Cincinnati fans stuff ballot boxes; most of the Reds regulars are voted All-Star starters. Commissioner Ford Frick disallows the vote and replaces some of the Reds with whom he deems more deserving players.

- Gold Glove Awards are originated, but only one is given at each position in 1957.

- The Giants' Willie Mays, Detroit's Al Kaline, and Minnie Minoso of the White Sox win the first three Gold Gloves for outfielders. Other Gold Gloves go to White Sox Nellie Fox (second base), Red Sox Frank Malzone (third), and Cincy's Roy McMillan (short). Remaining Gold Gloves go to Dodger Gil Hodges (first base), White Sox Sherm Lollar (catcher), and Yankee Bobby Shantz (pitcher).

> **"All I want out of life is that when I walk down the street people will say, 'There goes the greatest hitter who ever lived.'"**
>
> —*Boston's Ted Williams*

- Mays tops the NL in triples (20) and steals (38).

- Washington's Roy Sievers leads the AL in homers (42), RBI (114), and total bases (331).

- In their first full season under manager Fred Haney, the Braves defeat the Cards by eight games in the NL standings. The Dodgers slump to 11 games out.

- The Phillies become the last NL team to break the color line when they put John Kennedy in the infield.

- A new rule calls for a hitter to average 3.1 plate appearances per scheduled game to qualify for a batting title.

- The Yankees win the AL pennant for the third year in a row. The White Sox, after building an early lead over New York, find themselves eight games behind at season's end.

- The world championship leaves the Big Apple for the first time since 1948, as Atlanta goes seven games to knock off the Yankees. Milwaukee's Eddie Mathews hits a three-run homer to clinch a 7-5 win in the fourth game, a turning point in the Series. He also ends the final game, a 5-0 victory, with a diving stop.

- Brave Lew Burdette wins three complete games in the World Series, including two shutouts.

1958

Auto accident leaves Campanella paralyzed... Williams wins bat title at 40... Yanks storm back to win Series

- The Dodgers and Giants start the season in Los Angeles and San Francisco, respectively.

- Chicago's Ernie Banks is named NL MVP. Banks tops the NL in homers (47), RBI (129), total bases (379), runs produced (201), and SA (.614).

- Boston's Jackie Jensen is the AL MVP.

- Yankee Bob Turley wins the Cy Young and is second in the AL MVP vote. He leads the AL in wins (21) and winning pct. (.750) and ties in complete games (19).

- San Francisco's Orlando Cepeda is the unanimous choice as the NL's top rookie. He leads the NL in doubles (38) and hits .312 with 25 homers.

- St. Louis's Stan Musial becomes the first player since Paul Waner to collect 3,000 hits.

- Roy Campanella's career ends when he's left paralyzed by an auto accident.

- Richie Ashburn of the last-place Phillies tops the majors in BA (.350), hits (215), and triples (13) and leads the NL in walks (97) and OBP (.441). Ashburn also ties an NL record by leading outfielders in chances for the ninth time.

- Milwaukee's Warren Spahn and Pittsburgh's Bob Friend tie for the ML lead with 22 wins. Spahn tops the NL in complete games (23) and innings (290) and ties for the lead in winning pct. (.667).

Nellie Fox of the White Sox plays in a major-league record 98 consecutive games without striking out.

- Boston's Ted Williams wins the AL bat crown (.328) at age 40.

- On September 20, Oriole Hoyt Wilhelm wins his first game as a starting pitcher when he no-hits the Yankees.

- Gold Glove selections are made for the first time in both leagues.

- Willie Mays leads the NL in runs (121) and steals (31).

- Giant Stu Miller paces the NL in ERA (2.47).

- New York's Mickey Mantle leads the AL in homers (42), runs (127), runs produced (182), total bases (307), and walks (129).

- The Reds make just 100 errors to set an ML record.

- Yankee Ryne Duren tops the AL with 20 saves and fans 87 in just 75⅔ innings.

- Sam Jones of St. Louis becomes the first NL pitcher to fan 200 or more since 1941, setting down 225 batters on strikes.

- The Pirates are the surprise team in the NL, but they are still no match for Spahn, Hank Aaron, and the Braves. Milwaukee wins its second straight flag by eight games.

- Whitey Ford (AL ERA leader at 2.01) bounces back from a subpar year, combining with Turley and hitting star Mantle to help the Yanks win their eighth pennant in nine seasons. The second-place White Sox are a distant 10 games off the pace.

- Milwaukee and New York stage their second straight seven-game Series, and it looks dismal for the Yankees when they face a 3-1 deficit. One of their three losses comes by a lopsided 13-5 margin in Game 2.

- New York becomes the first team since the 1925 Pirates to overcome a 3-1 margin in the Series. It takes a 10-inning win to even the set, and the finale is a 6-2 game decided when the Bronx Bombers score four times in the eighth. Three of those final Series runs score on a Bill Skowron homer.

Mickey Mantle and Willie Mays

1959

Mr. Cub repeats as NL MVP... Baseball doubles its All-Star fun... City of Angels now city of champs

- Cub Ernie Banks repeats as NL MVP. He tops the ML in RBI but loses the NL homer crown to Milwaukee's Eddie Mathews (46 to 45). Banks sets NL shortstop marks with 143 RBI and a .985 FA.

- White Sox second baseman Nellie Fox is the AL MVP.

- The Braves' Hank Aaron tops the majors in BA at .355 and leads the NL in hits (223), total bases (400), SA (.636), and runs produced (200).

- Detroit's Harvey Kuenn hits .353 to lead the AL. He also paces the loop in hits (198) and doubles (42).

- White Sox Early Wynn leads the majors with 22 wins and takes the Cy Young Award.

- Joe Cronin is named AL president, making him the first former player to reach that pinnacle.

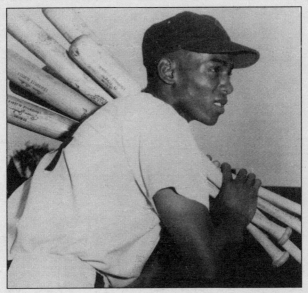

Ernie Banks

- Pumpsie Green is the first African-American player to join the Red Sox, the last ML team to break the color line.

- On August 31, Dodger Sandy Koufax becomes the first NL hurler in the 20th century to fan 18 in a game.

- Pirate Harvey Haddix pitches a record 12 perfect innings vs. Milwaukee on May 26, but he loses 1-0 in 13 innings.

- Boston's Jackie Jensen repeats as AL RBI champ (112) but hits no triples for the second year in a row.

- For the first time, there are two All-Star Games. The NL wins the first 5-4 at Pittsburgh, and the AL takes the second 5-3 at LA.

- Bill Veeck buys the White Sox.

- Cleveland's Rocky Colavito hits four homers on June 10.

- Elroy Face wins a season-record 17 straight games in relief (22 games over a two-year period). He finishes 18-1 with a .947 winning pct.

- Baltimore's Dave Philley collects a record nine consecutive pinch hits.

- Detroit's Eddie Yost tops the AL in runs (115), walks (135), and OBP (.437).

- Washington's Harmon Killebrew ties Colavito for the AL lead in homers (42).

- Ted Williams and Stan Musial both fail to hit .300 for the first time in their careers.

- A Roy Campanella Night exhibition game between the Yankees and Dodgers draws a record 93,103 fans to the LA Coliseum.

- Luis Aparicio of the Chicago White Sox leads the ML in stolen bases with 56.

- Willie McCovey of the Giants goes 4-for-4 in his debut, bats .354, and wins Rookie of the Year honors.

- New York fails to win the AL pennant for only the second time in 11 years. The loaded White Sox hand the Indians yet another second-place finish by five games.

- San Francisco holds a two-game lead over Los Angeles and Milwaukee with one week to go on the NL schedule. The Dodgers then sweep a three-game series in San Francisco en route to a first-place tie with the Braves.

- For the first time since leaving Brooklyn, the Dodgers win the NL pennant. They do so by sweeping a best-of-three playoff series against Milwaukee.

- Los Angeles gets its first World Series title with a six-game win over Chicago. The White Sox overcame a Coliseum crowd of 92,706 for a 1-0 win in Game 5, but the Dodgers wrap up the Series in Chicago.

- Larry Sherry of the Dodgers is Series MVP, winning two games and saving two others.

1960

Two teams join The Show... Williams homers in final at-bat... Maz's memorable blast powers Pirates

- Yankee Roger Maris is the AL MVP. Maris tops the AL in RBI (112) and SA (.581).

- Branch Rickey's proposed rival major league, the Continental League, forces the majors to expand for the first time since 1901. The AL grants expansion franchises for the 1961 season to Washington and Los Angeles. The AL also approves the transfer of the existing Washington franchise to Minneapolis-St. Paul.

- Lindy McDaniel of the Cards records 26 saves, an NL record.

- Pittsburgh's Vern Law goes 20-9 and wins the Cy Young Award.

- White Sox owner Bill Veeck is the first to put player names on the backs of his team's uniforms. Veeck also unveils the first exploding scoreboard.

- Pirate Dick Groat is named NL MVP.

- On April 17, Cleveland swaps Rocky Colavito to Detroit for Harvey Kuenn.

- Boston's Ted Williams hits his 500th homer on June 17. Williams homers in his last ML at-bat on September 28.

- San Francisco's Juan Marichal debuts on July 19 with a one-hit shutout of the Phils.

- On August 10, Detroit trades manager Jimmy Dykes for Cleveland manager Joe Gordon.

> **"He was as good as I've ever seen at turning the double play. They called him 'No Hands' because he threw so quickly he never seemed to touch the ball."**
>
> —*Don Kessinger on Pittsburgh's Bill Mazeroski*

- Orioles manager Paul Richards devises an oversized catcher's mitt to handle Hoyt Wilhelm's knucklers.

- The Cubs' Ernie Banks leads the majors with 41 homers.

- New York's Mickey Mantle leads the AL in homers (40), runs (119), and total bases (294).

- Milwaukee's Warren Spahn and Cardinal Ernie Broglio top the majors with 21 wins.

- For the first time in ML history, both batting leaders hit under .330.

- The Giants' Willie Mays wins his fourth consecutive Gold Glove.

- Detroit's Frank Lary tops the AL with 15 complete games—lowest total to this juncture to lead a league.

- Annual income from TV tops $12 million for the first time in ML history.

- With the doors now open in the big leagues, the last of the major Negro Leagues disbands after the season.

- Without a single pitcher posting more than 15 wins, the Yankees return to the top in the AL. They win their final 15 games of the season to stretch their margin to eight games over the Orioles.

- Danny Murtaugh's Pirates finish 95-59 in the NL, seven games better than the Braves. It's the team's first pennant since 1927.

- In the World Series, the Yankees outscore Pittsburgh 46-17 over the first six games but manage to win just three of them.

- Bill Mazeroski blasts a solo home run in the bottom of the ninth inning of the finale at Forbes Field clinching a drama-packed 10-9 Pittsburgh victory. It is the first World Series to end with a homer, and it gives the Pirates their first world title in 35 years.

- Manager Casey Stengel is fired after his World Series loss despite winning nine World Series in 12 seasons at the Yankee helm.

Bill Mazeroski after World Series home run

1961

Maris eclipses Ruth's long-ball record... Twins, Angels, eight games join AL... Spahn the first lefty to win 300

- AL now has 10 teams as the Minnesota Twins and Los Angeles Angels are added. The AL's season is expanded to 162 games.

- New York's Roger Maris is named AL MVP. Maris breaks Babe Ruth's ML season record by hitting 61 homers. Maris leads the AL in RBI (142) and total bases (366) and ties fellow Yankee Mickey Mantle for the lead in runs (132). Maris hits his 61st homer on the season's last day off Tracy Stallard of the Red Sox.

- Mantle hits 54 homers, giving him and Maris a teammate-record 115 four-baggers. The Yankees hit 240 homers to set an ML record. The team has six players who hit 20 or more homers, which also sets an ML record.

- The Giants' Willie Mays hits four homers on April 30 vs. the Braves.

Roger Maris, clubbing his 61st home run

- The Reds' Frank Robinson is named NL MVP.

- Cubs owner William Wrigley, tired of second-division finishes, has four coaches manage the team at various times of the year. They finish 64-90.

- Detroit's Norm Cash tops the expanded AL in batting with a .361 BA.

- Yankee Whitey Ford tops the majors with 25 victories and wins the Cy Young Award.

- Pittsburgh's Roberto Clemente wins his first NL bat crown (.351).

- The Phillies lose an ML-record 23 straight games.

- Giant Orlando Cepeda tops the NL with 46 homers and 142 RBI.

- Milwaukee's Warren Spahn leads the NL in wins for the eighth time, as he and the Reds' Joey Jay triumph 21 times. Spahn wins his 300th game—first NL southpaw to do so.

- The NL wins the first All-Star Game of the year, 5-4 in 10 innings at San Francisco. The second All-Star Game ends in a 1-1 tie at Boston, as rain stops play after nine innings.

- Ty Cobb dies on July 17.

- On May 9, Jim Gentile hits grand slams in two consecutive innings for Baltimore.

- The Braves hit four consecutive homers on June 8 vs. the Reds to set an ML record.

- The NL announces it will expand to 10 teams in 1962, placing franchises in New York and Houston.

- Baltimore's Dave Philley sets an ML record when he collects 24 pinch hits.

- Luis Arroyo of the Yankees sets an ML record when he notches 29 saves.

- Detroit rookie Jake Wood fans 141 times to set an ML record.

- Milwaukee's Eddie Mathews hits 30 or more homers for the ninth consecutive year to set an NL record.

- The Giants' Mays leads the NL in runs (129) and runs produced (212).

- The Reds cop their first pennant since 1940, beating the Dodgers by four games in the NL.

- The Yankees win 109 games in the new 162-game season, leaving the unfortunate Tigers in second place despite 101 victories.

- Cincinnati is no match for the Bronx Bombers in a five-game World Series. Ford wins twice without allowing an earned run. Bobby Richardson hits .391 and Bill Skowron .353. Maris bats only .105 and the injured Mantle gets one hit in six at-bats.

- Ford's shutout in the fourth game of the Series breaks Ruth's $29^{2/3}$ consecutive scoreless-inning streak in Series play. Ford leaves in the sixth inning, with a 32-inning streak intact, because of an ankle injury.

1962

Wills steals the show... Mets set failure record with 120 losses... Terry, Yanks blank Giants in Game 7

- Dodger Maury Wills is named NL MVP, edging out San Francisco's Willie Mays. Wills sets an ML record with 104 stolen bases.

- Yankee Mickey Mantle is named AL MVP. Mantle tops the AL in OBP (.488) and walks (122).

- Dodger Don Drysdale tops the majors with 25 wins and earns the Cy Young prize.

- Tommy Davis of LA wins the NL bat crown (.346) and knocks home 153 runs, most by anyone in the majors since 1949. Davis leads the majors with 230 hits and 246 runs produced.

- Mays leads the majors with 49 homers and 382 total bases.

- The expansion New York Mets amass 120 losses, a 20th-century ML record.

- Jackie Robinson becomes the first African-American player inducted into the Hall of Fame.

- Jack Sanford wins 16 straight games for the Giants.

- Twins slugger Harmon Killebrew tops the AL in homers (48), RBI (126), and SA (.545). Killebrew sets an ML record when he fans 142 times.

- The expansion Angels finish third in the AL, leading the loop as late as July 4.

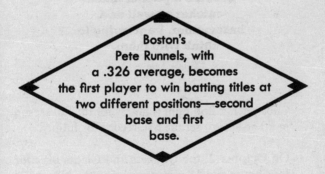

Boston's Pete Runnels, with a .326 average, becomes the first player to win batting titles at two different positions—second base and first base.

- Minnesota pitcher Jim Kaat wins his first of a record 14 consecutive Gold Gloves.

- On September 12 vs. Baltimore, Washington's Tom Cheney fans an ML-record 21 batters in a 16-inning game, winning 2-1.

- Five no-hitters are tossed during the year. The Angels' Bo Belinsky, Boston's Earl Wilson and Bill Monbouquette, the Dodgers' Sandy Koufax, and Minnesota's Jack Kralick blank their foes.

- Dodger Stadium opens on April 10, LA vs. Cincinnati.

- Pirates reliever Diomedes Olivo, age 43, is probably the oldest rookie in ML history.

> "Once I get on first, I become a pitcher and a catcher as well as a baserunner. I am trying to think with them."
>
> — *Dodger Maury Wills*

- Cubs pitcher Bob Buhl is hitless for the full season in 70 at-bats to set the ML record for futility.

- On October 2, the Dodgers and Giants play for four hours and 18 minutes, setting the NL record for longest nine-inning game.

- The Reds' Frank Robinson tops the majors in runs (134), doubles (51), and SA (.624), and he leads the NL in OBP (.424).

- Pirate Elroy Face sets an NL save record with 28.

- For the fourth time since 1946, the Dodgers are involved in a pennant playoff. For the third time, they lose, falling to the Giants in a best-of-three set after losing 10 of their last 13 regular-season games. San Francisco overcomes a 4-2 deficit in the deciding game to win the pennant.

- The Yanks win their third consecutive AL flag, five games ahead of Killebrew and the Twins.

- Whitey Ford's scoreless inning streak in Series play is stopped at 33⅔ when the Giants score in the second inning of his opening-game win. The Yankees take a 3-2 lead before the Series is delayed by three straight days of rain.

- The Giants force a seventh game at San Francisco, which Yankee Bill Terry wins 1-0 over Sanford. With runners at second and third and two outs in the bottom of the ninth inning, New York second baseman Bobby Richardson snares a hard line drive by Willie McCovey to clinch the title.

1963

Koufax, Dodgers blow away Yanks... Howard baseball's first African-American MVP... Yaz cops AL bat crown

- Dodger Sandy Koufax is named NL MVP. Koufax is also the first unanimous choice for the Cy Young Award. He sets a modern NL record with 306 Ks and a modern ML record for southpaws with 11 shutouts.

- Yankee Elston Howard becomes the first African-American player to win AL MVP honors.

- Milwaukee's Hank Aaron leads the majors in runs (121), RBI (130), total bases (370), SA (.586), and runs produced (207). Aaron ties the Giants' Willie McCovey for the NL homer crown (44).

- Boston's Carl Yastrzemski wins his first AL bat crown (.321). Yaz also leads the AL in hits (183), doubles (40), walks (95), and OBP (.419).

- Minnesota's Harmon Killebrew leads the AL in homers (45) and SA (.555).

Sandy Koufax

- LA's Tommy Davis repeats as NL bat champ (.326).

- Roger Craig of the Mets loses 18 consecutive games. Craig finishes with a 5-22 record and suffers nine shutout losses, most by any NL hurler since 1908. The Mets lose 22 straight games on the road to set a modern ML record.

- Milwaukee's Warren Spahn breaks Eddie Plank's record for most career wins by a southpaw when he collects his 328th victory. Spahn, at age 42, becomes the oldest 20-game winner in history when he goes 23-7 for the Braves.

- White Sox Dave Nicholson fans 175 times, breaking the ML record by 33.

- The Twins crush 225 home runs—second most in ML history.

- Boston reliever Dick Radatz has 25 saves, a 15-6 record, and 162 Ks in 132⅓ innings for a seventh-place team.

- Cincinnati's Pete Rose wins the NL Rookie of the Year prize.

- On September 13, the three Alou brothers briefly play together in the outfield for the Giants in the same game.

- On July 31, Cleveland becomes the first AL team to hit four consecutive homers. All are off Angel Paul Foytack.

- Stan Musial retires as the holder of NL records for games (3,026), at-bats (10,972), hits (3,630), RBI (1,951), runs (1,949), and doubles (725) (all since broken).

- Early Wynn wins his 300th game on July 13.

- The Polo Grounds, now home of the Mets, finishes its final season as a major-league ballpark. More than a million fans attend games despite a 111-loss season for the home team.

- Rogers Hornsby dies on January 5.

- On June 9 in Houston, the Colt .45s beat the Giants in the first Sunday night game in major-league history.

- Maury Wills and Luis Aparicio again are stolen-base kings, each with 40.

- The Dodgers sweep a key three-game series in St. Louis late in the season to pull away from the Cardinals by six games for the NL pennant.

- The Yankees, despite prolonged injuries to Mickey Mantle and Roger Maris, have little trouble winning 104 games and their fourth AL flag in a row. Whitey Ford wins a league-best 24 games.

- New York is swept in the World Series for the first time since 1924. Koufax outpitches Ford in the first and fourth games of the set, striking out a Series-record 15 batters in the 5-2 opener and eight more hitters in the 2-1 finale. He wins Series MVP honors.

Oliva makes dashing debut...Hapless Mets open Shea Stadium...Cards hand Yanks second straight Series loss

- St. Louis's Ken Boyer is named the NL MVP.

- Brooks Robinson of Baltimore cops the AL MVP Award.

- Tony Oliva of the Twins is named AL Rookie of the Year after winning the bat title (.323). Oliva leads the majors and sets an AL rookie record for hits (217). He also tops the majors in total bases (374) and the AL in runs (109) and doubles (43).

- Wally Bunker, age 19, wins 19 games for the Orioles—most in the 20th century by a teenage pitcher.

- Boston's Dick Radatz has 16 wins and an ML-high 29 saves for a team that wins only 72 games.

- On May 31, the Mets and Giants play a twin bill that lasts nine hours, 52 minutes—an ML record.

- Philly's Dick Allen is named NL Rookie of the Year, as he tops the loop in total bases with 352—an NL rookie record—and runs (125) and ties in triples (13).

- New York's Shea Stadium opens on April 17—the Mets vs. Pittsburgh. The Mets finish last for the third consecutive year under Casey Stengel, losing an ML-record 340 games over a three-year period.

- Jim Bunning pitches a perfect game vs. the Mets on June 21—the first perfect game in the NL in the 20th century.

- Houston's Ken Johnson becomes the first ML hurler to lose a complete game no-hitter in nine innings, as the Reds beat him 1-0 on April 23.

- Boston's Tony Conigliaro, age 19, hits 24 homers and has a .530 SA—both records for a teenage player.

- Baltimore's Luis Aparicio leads the AL in steals (57) for the ninth consecutive year.

- Johnny Wyatt of KC is the first pitcher in ML history to appear in at least half of his team's games (81 of 162).

- LA's Dean Chance leads the AL in ERA (1.65), shutouts (11), innings pitched (278), and complete games (15).

- The Giants' Willie Mays tops the NL in homers (47) and SA (.607).

- LA's Sandy Koufax no-hits the Phils on June 4. It's his third no-no in three years. He also Ks 18 Cubs on April 24. Koufax is held to 223 innings by arm

Brooks Robinson

trouble, but he still leads the NL in shutouts (seven), winning pct. (.792), and ERA (1.74).

- Yankee Mickey Mantle is awarded baseball's first $100,000 contract.

- Ken Hubbs of the Cubs dies in a private plane crash before the season.

- The Cardinals win a tight race for the NL pennant after four teams enter the final weekend with a chance to win. The Phillies squander a 6½-game lead with two weeks to go, tying the Reds for second place by a single game. Only three games separate the top four teams.

- The Yankees also make up a 6½-game deficit by finishing 30-10, overtaking the White Sox by one. No pitcher wins as many as 19 games on New York's fifth consecutive pennant winner.

- St. Louis outlasts the Yankees in seven games, handing New York its first back-to-back Series setbacks since 1921-22. Tim McCarver of the Cardinals leads all hitters with a .478 average.

- Cardinal pitcher Bob Gibson strikes out 13 men in a 10-inning win in Game 5, then comes back on two days' rest to prevail 7-5 in the finale. Bobby Richardson racks up a Series-record 13 hits for the Yankees.

Twins give Minnesota a pennant... Paige handcuffs A's at age 65... Koufax, Dodgers reign supreme

- The Giants' Willie Mays is named NL MVP. Mays leads the majors in homers (52), total bases (360), SA (.645), and OBP (.399). He also smacks an NL-record 17 homers in a month.

- Minnesota's Zoilo Versalles is chosen AL MVP over teammate Tony Oliva. Versalles tops the AL in runs (126) and total bases (308) and ties for the lead in doubles (45) and triples (19).

- For the second time, Dodger Sandy Koufax is a unanimous choice for the Cy Young Award, as he Ks 382 to set an ML record. Koufax tops the majors with 26 wins, a .765 winning pct., 336 innings, 27 complete games, and a 2.04 ERA. He pitches a perfect game and his fourth no-hitter in four years, beating Chicago 1-0 on September 9.

- The Mets lose 112 games for a four-year ML record of 452 losses.

- Baseball adopts an annual free-agent (rookie) draft. The Kansas City A's select Rick Monday with the No. 1 pick.

- The Yankees open the season with Johnny Keane as manager, having replaced Yogi Berra following the previous campaign.

- Jim Maloney of the Reds pitches a no-hitter for 10 innings over the Mets on June 14 but loses in 11 innings. Maloney then goes 10 innings to win a no-hitter, 1-0 over Chicago on August 19.

- At 65, Satchel Paige becomes the oldest to play in an ML game when he hurls three scoreless innings for KC vs. Boston on September 25.

> **"Pitching is the art of instilling fear by making a man flinch."**
>
> —*Dodger Sandy Koufax*

- Ted Abernathy's 31 saves for the Cubs set an ML record.

- Bert Campaneris plays all nine positions for the A's on September 8.

- Spike Eckert replaces Ford Frick as baseball's commissioner.

- The first indoor stadium, the Astrodome, opens on April 9—Houston vs. Yankees in an exhibition game.

- Oliva again leads the AL in batting (.321) and also leads in hits (185) and runs produced (189).

- Boston's Carl Yastrzemski tops the AL in OBP (.398) and SA (.536) and ties for the lead in doubles (45).

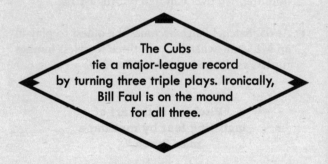

The Cubs tie a major-league record by turning three triple plays. Ironically, Bill Faul is on the mound for all three.

- Boston's Tony Conigliaro leads the AL with 32 homers, and at 20 is the youngest ever to win a league homer crown.

- Emmett Ashford makes his debut as the first African-American umpire in the majors.

- The great career of Warren Spahn comes to an end after 21 years in the majors.

- Cleveland's Sam McDowell leads the AL in ERA (2.18) and sets an AL southpaw record for Ks (325).

- The Twins win their franchise's first AL pennant since 1933. The five-time defending Yankees finish in sixth place, while Minnesota finishes seven games ahead of the White Sox. Harmon Killebrew is one of three Twins players to hit more than 20 home runs (leading the team with 25).

- The Dodgers edge the Giants by two games for the NL flag. In two key situations, LA uses Koufax in relief. He earns a save each time.

- LA manager Walter Alston wins an NL-record fourth World Series, as the Dodgers rally for a seven-game triumph after losing the first two games in Minnesota.

- Koufax earns two complete-game victories in the Series, including a 2-0 decision against Jim Kaat in the deciding game at Minnesota. He strikes out 29 batters in three Series games. Ron Fairly leads LA with a .379 average, 11 hits, and six RBI.

1966

Koufax wins 27, then retires ... Robinson takes Triple Crown ... Orioles sweep Series from Dodgers

- Baltimore's Frank Robinson is named AL MVP after winning the Triple Crown (.316, 49, 122). Robinson also leads the AL in runs (122), total bases (367), runs produced (195), OBP (.415), and SA (.637).

- An arthritic elbow forces Sandy Koufax to retire after the season. In his final campaign, Koufax tops the majors with 27 wins, 27 complete games, 317 Ks, and 323 innings. He also leads the NL in ERA an all-time record fifth consecutive time with a 1.73 mark. Koufax wins his third unanimous Cy Young Award in the last four years.

- Prior to the season, Koufax and Don Drysdale stage the first dual holdout by teammates in ML history.

- The Yankees tumble into the cellar for the first time since 1912.

- Pittsburgh's Roberto Clemente is named NL MVP.

- Marvin Miller is elected president of the Major League Baseball Players Association.

- Pitcher Tony Cloninger of the Braves hits two grand slams in a game on July 3.

- On May 1, Angel Bobby Knoop participates in a single-game record six double plays by a second baseman.

Frank Robinson

- The Braves move to Atlanta. The first game in Dixie is on April 12 at Fulton County Stadium, Pirates vs. Braves.

- Pittsburgh's Matty Alou leads the NL in BA (.342); brother Felipe Alou of Atlanta is second (.327). Felipe leads the NL in runs (122) and total bases (355) and tops the majors in hits (218).

- Minnesota's Tony Oliva tops the AL in hits for the third time in his three major-league seasons, as he collects 191 in '66.

> **"When I'm 40 years old, I'd still like to be able to comb my hair."**
>
> —*Sandy Koufax, explaining why he quit baseball at age 30 with an arthritic elbow*

- Cards rookie Larry Jaster ties for the NL lead in shutouts with five, all against the Dodgers.

- The first game in Anaheim Stadium is on April 19, White Sox vs. Angels.

- The first game in Busch Stadium is on May 12, Braves vs. Cards.

- Jack Aker's 32 saves for KC set an ML record.

- The Braves' Hank Aaron paces the NL in homers (44) and the majors in RBI (127) and runs produced (200).

- The Giants' Juan Marichal wins 25 and tops the majors in winning pct. (.806).

- The AL has only two hitters above .288—Robinson (.316) and Oliva (.307).

- Minnesota's Jim Kaat leads the AL with 25 wins, 305 innings, and 19 complete games.

- Paced by the power of Frank Robinson, Brooks Robinson, and Boog Powell in the middle of the order, along with a deep pitching staff, the Orioles are the class of the AL. The defending champion Twins wind up nine games behind in second place.

- The Dodgers repeat in the NL, but not without a scare from the Giants. LA clinches on the next-to-last day of the season, when Koufax wins the second game of a doubleheader with the Phillies.

- The World Series ends in a flash, with Baltimore sweeping LA in four games and holding the Dodgers scoreless for the final 33 innings. The score of the opener is 5-2, but the final three games are shutouts.

- The Orioles score their only runs in the third and fourth games of the Series on homers by Paul Blair and Frank Robinson, respectively.

1967

Yaz wins Triple Crown... Mantle, Mathews smash 500th homers... Red Sox soar to first before Series setback

- Boston's Carl Yastrzemski is the near-unanimous AL MVP after winning the last Triple Crown of the 20th century (.326, 44, 121). Yaz also leads the AL in runs (112), hits (189), total bases (360), runs produced (189), OBP (.421), and SA (.622).

- St. Louis's Orlando Cepeda wins the NL MVP Award.

- Tom Seaver wins a club-record 16 games for the Mets and is named NL Rookie of the Year.

- Minnesota's Rod Carew wins AL Rookie of the Year honors.

- Al Kaline wins the last of his 10 Gold Gloves as an AL outfielder.

- Yankee Mickey Mantle hits his 500th homer on May 13.

- Boston's Tony Conigliaro is beaned by Angel Jack Hamilton. His vision is impaired and he'll be out of the game until 1969.

- The Red Sox jump from ninth place in 1966 to first in '67—the first team to do so in the 20th century.

- Two Cy Young Awards are given for the first time. Boston's Jim Lonborg is an easy winner in the AL. San Francisco's Mike McCormick wins the NL Cy Young after leading the loop with 22 wins.

- The NL wins the longest game in All-Star history, 2-1 in 15 innings at Anaheim, as the Reds' Tony Perez homers to win it.

- The Mets trade Bill Denehy and $100,000 to Washington in order to obtain Gil Hodges as their manager.

- On April 30, Orioles Steve Barber and Stu Miller lose a combined no-hitter to Detroit, 2-1 in nine innings.

- Whitey Ford retires with a .690 career winning pct., best in the 20th century among 200-game winners.

- Only able to pitch weekends because of his military service obligation, the Cubs' Kenny Holtzman nonetheless posts a 9-0 record.

Carl Yastrzemski

- Cleveland pitchers fan an AL-record 1,189 hitters.

- Houston's Eddie Mathews hits his 500th homer on July 14.

- Pittsburgh's Roberto Clemente leads the majors with 209 hits and 190 runs produced.

- Atlanta's Hank Aaron leads the NL in homers (39), SA (.573), and total bases (344) and ties for the lead in runs (113).

- White Sox pitchers Joe Horlen, Gary Peters, and Tommy John finish one-two-four, respectively, in ERA in the AL, with Horlen checking in at 2.06.

- The AL's BA is down to .236, as the Red Sox are the only team to hit above .243.

- Jimmie Foxx dies on July 21.

- The rise of the Red Sox culminates in a one-game AL pennant victory over Minnesota and Detroit. The Tigers have a chance to force a playoff by sweeping a final-day doubleheader with California, but they lose the second game 8-5.

- St. Louis wins 101 games in running away with the NL pennant. The Cardinals clinch with two weeks to go in the season, as Bob Gibson returns from a broken leg suffered 52 days earlier to three-hit the Phillies.

- Cardinal Lou Brock hits .414 in the World Series, steals a Series-record seven bases, and scores eight runs to lead St. Louis to the championship in seven games.

- Gibson's Series numbers include three complete-game wins, a 1.00 ERA, and 26 strikeouts in 27 innings. He throws a three-hitter to win the finale by a 7-2 score.

1968

Gibson gets downright dominant... McLain reaches 30-win plateau... Tigers pull off unlikely Series comeback

- St. Louis's Bob Gibson posts a 1.12 ERA, lowest in the ML since 1914, and is named the NL's MVP and Cy Young winner. He also has 13 shutouts, most in the ML since 1916.

- Detroit's Denny McLain, the first 30-game winner in the ML since 1934, cops both the AL MVP and Cy Young honors by racking up 31 wins.

- The A's move to Oakland and top the AL with a .240 BA, lowest in ML history by a loop leader.

- Houston beats the Mets 1-0 in 24 innings on April 15, making it the longest 1-0 game in ML history.

- LA's Don Drysdale sets a new ML record when he pitches 58 consecutive scoreless innings.

- Luis Tiant Ks 19 batters for Cleveland in a 10-inning game on July 3.

- Boston's Carl Yastrzemski wins the AL bat crown with a .301 BA, lowest in ML history to lead a league.

- The Yankees set a post-dead-ball era record for lowest team batting average when they hit just .214.

- The NL wins the first indoor All-Star Game, 1-0 at Houston, as the winning run scores on a double-play grounder. The Giants' Willie Mays becomes the first player to win two All-Star MVP Awards.

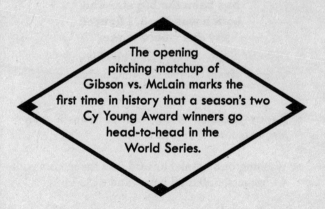

The opening pitching matchup of Gibson vs. McLain marks the first time in history that a season's two Cy Young Award winners go head-to-head in the World Series.

- The Player Relations Committee and the Players Association hammer out their first "Basic Agreement."

- Cesar Tovar plays all nine positions for the Twins on September 22.

- Giant Jim Davenport's ML-record streak of 97 consecutive errorless games at third base ends.

- Atlanta's Hank Aaron hits his 500th homer on July 14.

- On July 29, Washington's Ron Hansen performs an unassisted triple play vs. Cleveland.

> **"All my life somebody else has been the big star and Lolich was No. 2. I figured my day would come."**
>
> —*Tiger Mickey Lolich after being named MVP of the World Series*

- Randy Hundley of the Cubs catches a major-league record 160 games.

- Washington's Frank Howard tops the majors with 44 homers, 330 total bases, and a .552 SA.

- San Francisco's Willie McCovey leads the NL in homers (36), RBI (105), and SA (.545).

- The Giants' Juan Marichal tops the NL in wins (26), complete games (30), and innings (326).

- On May 8, Catfish Hunter of the A's pitches a perfect game vs. the Twins and collects three hits and three RBI in his own cause.

- With the masterful McLain leading the way, the Tigers run off with the AL pennant by 12 games over the Orioles.

- The NL flag chase is also a one-sided affair, with Gibson and the Cardinals topping the Giants by nine contests.

- What shapes up as a classic Series lives up to its billing. Favored St. Louis wins three of the first four games, including Gibson's 17-strikeout performance (a Series record) in the opener. Detroit takes the next two to set up a seventh game.

- In the deciding Series contest, an outfield misplay by Cardinal Curt Flood and the five-hit pitching of Mickey Lolich stake the Tigers to a 4-1 triumph and the world title. It is Lolich's third win of the Series.

- Lou Brock of St. Louis tops all World Series batters with a .464 BA and a record-tying seven steals.

"Miracle Mets" *enjoy ride of a lifetime... Divisional playoffs added to postseason... Baseball expands into Canada*

- The AL and NL both expand to 12 teams and divide into two divisions, with division winners to play best-of-five playoffs. The four new teams are the San Diego Padres and Montreal Expos in the NL and Kansas City Royals and Seattle Pilots in the AL.

- On April 14 in the first ML game played outside of the United States, Montreal beats the Cards 8-7 at Jarry Park.

- Bowie Kuhn becomes baseball's new commissioner, replacing Spike Eckert.

- The Mets' Tom Seaver tops the majors with 25 wins and cops the Cy Young Award.

- The Twins' Harmon Killebrew leads the majors with 49 homers and 140 RBI and is named AL MVP.

- To add more offense, rules are made to reduce the height of the pitcher's mound and the size of the strike zone. The NL's BA jumps seven points; the AL's 16.

- The Giants' Willie McCovey is named NL MVP after leading the league in homers (45), RBI (126), SA (.656), and OBP (.458). McCovey receives an ML-record 45 intentional walks.

- By bunting his way on base in his last at-bat of the season, Pete Rose of the Reds breaks a tie with Roberto Clemente and wins the NL batting title (.348).

> **"They called us 'The Miracle Mets.' Miracle, my eye. What happened was a lot of good young players suddenly jelled and matured all at once."**
>
> —*The Mets' Tom Seaver*

- Detroit's Denny McLain leads the AL with nine shutouts and 24 wins. McLain and Baltimore's Mike Cuellar share the AL's Cy Young Award.

- Minnesota's Rod Carew steals home seven times to tie the ML season record.

- Baltimore's Dave McNally sets a franchise record by winning 15 games in a row.

- Ted Williams is hired as Washington's manager. The team finishes over .500 for the first time in its nine-year history.

- The Curt Flood case begins vs. organized baseball after Flood is traded to the Phils by the Cards and refuses to report to his new team.

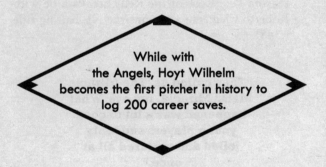

While with the Angels, Hoyt Wilhelm becomes the first pitcher in history to log 200 career saves.

- Twins manager Billy Martin beats up one of his own pitchers, Dave Boswell.

- LA's Willie Davis hits in 31 consecutive games.

- Houston hurlers fan an ML-record 1,221 hitters.

- Wayne Granger of the Reds becomes the first pitcher to appear in 90 games.

- Bobby Bonds of the Giants fans 187 times, setting an ML record.

- Jim Maloney of Cincinnati no-hits Houston on April 30. The next day, Houston's Don Wilson no-hits Cincinnati.

- On September 15 vs. the Mets, St. Louis's Steve Carlton strikes out an ML-record 19 batters.

- The New York Mets become the second team in three years to win a pennant after finishing as low as ninth place the previous year. They do it by overtaking the Cubs in dramatic style, winning 38 of their final 49 games while Chicago hits a September skid.

- The Braves win the NL West, but they are swept in three games in the first NLCS.

- The initial ALCS goes to AL East champion Baltimore, also in a sweep. The Orioles knock off AL West winner Minnesota.

- The "Miracle Mets" beat heavily favored Baltimore in five games in the World Series, earning a place in sports history as one of the most unlikely champions. Jerry Koosman wins two Series games and posts an ERA of 2.04.

Mays, Aaron join 3,000 club... Milwaukee returns to big leagues... Orioles ride home run barrage to title

- The Seattle franchise is moved to Milwaukee just prior to the season. The team name is changed from Pilots to Brewers.

- Boog Powell of Baltimore is the AL MVP.

- The Reds' Johnny Bench is named NL MVP. Bench tops the majors in homers (45) and RBI (148).

- St. Louis's Bob Gibson wins his second NL Cy Young Award, as he ties the Giants' Gaylord Perry for the NL lead in wins (23).

- Minnesota's Jim Perry is the AL Cy Young winner, as he ties two others for the AL lead in wins (24). The Perrys are the first brothers to top their respective leagues in victories.

- The Orioles win 108 games, giving them 217 victories over the last two years.

- Atlanta's Rico Carty leads the ML with a .366 BA. He hits in 31 straight games.

- Angel Alex Johnson wins the AL batting title (.329) by a fraction of a point over Boston's Carl Yastrzemski.

- On April 22, Tom Seaver sets an ML record when he fans 10 Padres in a row and ties the ML record by fanning 19 total.

Johnny Bench

- Cub Billy Williams sets an NL record when he plays in his 1,117th consecutive game. Williams tops the ML in runs (137), total bases (373), and runs produced (224) and ties for the ML lead in hits (205).

- The Giants' Willie Mays collects his 3,000th hit.

- The NL wins its eighth straight All-Star Game, 5-4 in 12 innings at Cincinnati.

- Cincinnati's Wayne Granger sets an ML record with 35 saves.

- Giant Bobby Bonds fans 189 times to set an ML record.

- Three Rivers Stadium opens on July 16, the Reds vs. Pirates.

- Riverfront Stadium opens on June 30, the Braves vs. Reds.

- The Conigliaro brothers, Tony and Billy, hit 54 homers for the Red Sox.

- Cardinal Vic Davalillo ties the ML record with 24 pinch hits.

- Detroit's Cesar Gutierrez becomes the first player in the 20th century to go 7-for-7 when he accomplishes it on June 21 in a 12-inning game.

- Atlanta's Hank Aaron gets his 3,000th hit.

- Washington's Frank Howard leads the AL in homers (44), RBI (126), and walks (132).

- Umpires refuse to work LCS games and force a settlement that increases their salaries and benefits.

- Detroit's Denny McLain is suspended for part of the season for his involvement in a bookmaking operation. After the season, he is traded to Washington.

- The Orioles treat manager Earl Weaver to a second consecutive AL flag. They run away in the AL East, then sweep AL West champion Minnesota for the second straight year in the playoffs.

- The NLCS is also a sweep for the second time in as many years of existence. The Reds bounce the Pirates from the playoffs after easily winning their division.

- Baltimore socks 10 home runs in a five-game World Series triumph. The Reds' only win breaks a 17-game Oriole winning streak that spanned the end of the regular season, ALCS, and first three games of the Series.

- Brooks Robinson, with a .429 batting average and brilliant defense, wins the Series MVP Award.

*A's leave hitters feeling Blue...
Clemente's Bucs win it all...Series game
played under lights*

- Cardinal Joe Torre is named NL MVP, as he leads the league in BA (.363), hits (230), RBI (137), and total bases (352).

- Oakland's Vida Blue wins both the MVP and Cy Young Awards in the AL. Blue fans 301 in his first full ML season. He goes 24-8 and leads the AL in ERA (1.82) and shutouts (eight).

- Chicago's Ferguson Jenkins cops the NL Cy Young, as he leads the loop in wins (24), complete games (30), and innings (325).

- Tiger Mickey Lolich leads the AL in wins (25), innings (376), complete games (29), and Ks (308). Lolich's 45 starts and 376 innings are the most by any hurler since the dead-ball era.

- Pittsburgh's Willie Stargell leads the majors with 48 homers.

- Bill Melton of the White Sox tops the AL in homers with 33.

- Expo Ron Hunt sets the modern ML record when he's hit by pitches 50 times.

- The Astros play an ML-record 75 one-run games.

- Veterans Stadium opens on April 10, the Expos vs. Phils.

- Phillie Larry Bowa's .987 FA sets an ML record for shortstops.

- Cleveland third baseman Graig Nettles compiles an ML-record 412 assists.

- The Twins' Tony Oliva wins his third AL bat crown (.337).

- Atlanta's Earl Williams, a catcher/third baseman, hits 33 homers, an NL rookie record for both catchers and infielders.

- Phillie rookie Willie Montanez cracks 30 homers.

- Batting helmets become mandatory in both leagues.

- Houston's J.R. Richard ties Karl Spooner's major-league record when he strikes out 15 batters in his first start.

Roberto Clemente

- On June 23, Rick Wise of the Phils no-hits Cincinnati and hits two homers.

- St. Louis's Lou Brock tops the majors in runs (126) and steals (64).

- Minnesota's Harmon Killebrew leads the AL in RBI (119) and walks (114).

- The Mets' Tom Seaver tops the NL in Ks (289) and ERA (1.76), winning 20 games.

- Baltimore trades Frank Robinson and Pete Richert to the Dodgers for four players.

- The Mets trade Nolan Ryan and three others to the Angels for Jim Fregosi.

- Reds manager Sparky Anderson suffers a losing season (79-83). It will be his last sub-.500 campaign until 1989.

- The Orioles become the only flag winner in ML history to have four 20-game winners.

- Baltimore's AL pennant comes at the expense of the A's, who are the third straight ALCS sweep victims of the Orioles. Blue loses the opener to Dave McNally.

- The NL features the first LCS to go beyond the minimum three games, as the Giants extend the Pirates to four before falling. It is a sweep of sorts, as the Bucs take the final three games after dropping the opener.

- Game 4 at Pittsburgh is the first night game in World Series history. Before 51,378 fans, Roberto Clemente gets three hits and leads the Pirates to a 4-3 victory to tie the Series.

- The Bucs go on to win in seven games. Steve Blass finishes with two complete-game wins for the champs.

- Pittsburgh's Roberto Clemente is the overall Series star, hitting .414 with 12 hits and two homers.

1972

Players opt to call their own strike... Tenace nets A's a Series crown... Plane crash claims Clemente

- The Washington franchise moves to Texas and is renamed the Rangers.

- Cincinnati's Johnny Bench wins his second NL MVP Award. Bench leads the majors in homers (40) and RBI (125).

- Chicago's Dick Allen is named AL MVP. Allen leads the AL in homers (37), RBI (113), runs produced (166), OBP (.422), and SA (.603).

- Steve Carlton wins 27 of Philly's 59 victories and cops Cy Young honors. Carlton leads the majors in wins and complete games (30) and tops the NL in Ks (310), innings (346), and ERA (1.97).

- Mets manager Gil Hodges dies of a heart attack.

- The Cubs' Billy Williams tops the majors in BA (.333), SA (.606), and total bases (348).

- Cleveland's Gaylord Perry wins the AL Cy Young after tying for the loop lead in wins (24) and leading in complete games (29).

- The first players strike in ML history ends on April 10. Missed games are not made up, and Boston loses to the Tigers by a half-game.

- Pittsburgh's Roberto Clemente produces his 3,000th hit on September 30, then dies in a plane crash on December 31.

The Phillies' Steve Carlton sets a record for most consecutive wins by a pitcher on a last-place team when he racks up 15 straight victories.

- The NL wins its 10th straight All-Star Game, 4-3 in 10 innings at Atlanta.

- On September 2, Cub Milt Pappas no-hits the Padres. Pappas loses the perfect game by walking the 27th man on a 3-2 pitch.

- Jackie Robinson dies of a heart attack at age 53.

- Boston catcher Carlton Fisk is a unanimous choice for AL Rookie of the Year.

- Detroit's Ed Brinkman sets a new ML fielding-average record for shortstops (.990) and has 72 straight errorless games.

- Tiger Al Kaline's AL-record streak of 242 consecutive errorless games in the outfield ends.

- Rod Carew wins the AL bat title (.318). He is the first bat crown winner to go homerless since Zach Wheat in 1918.

- The Giants' Jim Barr retires an ML-record 41 batters in a row over a two-game period.

- On August 1, Padre Nate Colbert hits an ML record-tying five homers in a doubleheader and collects an ML-record 13 RBI.

- California's Nolan Ryan tops the AL in Ks (329) and sets an ML record by allowing only 5.26 hits per nine innings.

- Oakland ends Baltimore's reign in the AL by winning its first pennant since 1931. The A's do it with a Game 5 ALCS triumph over the pesky Tigers. Blue Moon Odom and Vida Blue combine on the 2-1 Game 5 victory.

- The NL also features an exciting pennant battle. The NL West champion Reds score twice in the bottom of the ninth inning for a 4-3 win in Game 5 to take the NLCS over Pittsburgh. Bench's home run ties the game, and the winning run scores on a Bob Moose wild pitch.

> **"Carlton does not pitch to the hitter; he pitches through him. The batter hardly exists for Steve. He's playing an elevated game of catch."**
>
> —Tim McCarver

- True to form in this postseason, the World Series goes the distance. Oakland's Gene Tenace homers in his first two at-bats and goes on to hit .348 with four home runs and nine RBI.

- Tenace's two hits and two RBI in the finale push the A's to a 3-2 win in Cincinnati. Catfish Hunter gets the victory in relief.

1973

Break-even Mets push A's to limit... Sox go with Wood again and again... Ryan fans a record 383 batters

- Oakland's Reggie Jackson is voted AL MVP, leading the loop in homers (32), RBI (117), runs (99), SA (.531), and runs produced (184).

- The Reds' Pete Rose cops NL MVP honors. Rose wins the bat crown (.338) and leads the majors in hits (230).

- The Mets' Tom Seaver is voted the Cy Young winner in the NL even though he wins just 19 games, five less than Ron Bryant of the Giants. Seaver leads the NL in ERA (2.08) and Ks (251) and ties for the lead in complete games (18).

- Baltimore's Jim Palmer wins his first Cy Young Award in the AL.

- The third "Basic Agreement" gives players the right to salary arbitration and to the "five and 10" rule with respect to trades.

- The AL adopts the designated hitter rule; pitchers no longer have to bat for themselves. On April 6, Yankee Ron Blomberg becomes the first DH to bat in an ML game.

- The Pirates' Willie Stargell tops the ML in homers (44), doubles (43), RBI (119), and SA (.646).

- George Steinbrenner buys the Yankees.

- White Sox Wilbur Wood is the first pitcher in 57 years to both win and lose 20 games in a season, as he goes 24-20 and ties Bryant for the ML lead in wins. On July 20, Wood becomes the last ML hurler to start both games of a doubleheader; he loses both.

> **"There are only two places in this league: first place and no place."**
>
> —*Tom Seaver*

- Oriole Bobby Grich's .995 fielding average sets an ML record for second basemen.

- Detroit reliever John Hiller sets an ML record with 38 saves.

- Yankee pitchers Mike Kekich and Fritz Peterson swap wives, families, houses, and pets.

- California's Nolan Ryan fans an ML-record 383 batters. Ryan no-hits KC on May 15 and Detroit on July 15.

- The Braves have three men with at least 40 homers—Dave Johnson (43), Darrell Evans (41), and Hank Aaron (40).

- The NL wins the All-Star Game 7-1 at Kansas City, as a record 54 players participate.

- The Twins' Rod Carew leads the AL in BA (.350) and hits (203) and ties for the lead in triples (11).

With the DH rule in place, the AL records 167 more complete games than the NL.

- Giant Bobby Bonds just misses becoming the first "40-40" player in ML history, as he hits 39 homers and steals 43 bases.

- The Mets win the NL flag despite posting a .509 winning pct., lowest of any pennant winner in history. No one else in the NL East has a winning record. The West champion Reds fall in five games in the NLCS to a Mets staff that notches a 1.33 ERA. The set features a brawl in Game 3.

- Oakland repeats its AL pennant. The A's beat Kansas City by six games in the AL West, then need the full five ALCS games to turn back Baltimore. Catfish Hunter shuts out the O's 3-0 in the fifth game.

- New York stretches the Series to its limit before falling to the powerful A's. Reserve second baseman Mike Andrews of the A's is dropped from the team by owner Charles O. Finley after his two errors help the Mets to a Game 2 win. Commissioner Bowie Kuhn reinstates him.

- The A's win the final two Series games at home for their second straight world title. Met Rusty Staub tops all batters in the World Series with 11 hits, a .423 BA, and six RBI.

- Oakland manager Dick Williams leaves the team after the Series.

1974

Aaron breaks Ruth's hallowed HR mark ... Brock burns up basepaths ... Oakland juggernaut rolls on

- Dodger Steve Garvey is named NL MVP.

- Ranger Jeff Burroughs wins the AL MVP Award, topping the loop in RBI (118) and runs produced (177).

- Atlanta's Hank Aaron hits his 715th career homer on April 8 off Al Downing of the Dodgers to set the all-time ML record. Aaron defeats Japanese slugger Sadaharu Oh 10-9 in a specially arranged home run contest in Tokyo.

- Phillie Mike Schmidt tops the majors with 36 homers.

- St. Louis's Lou Brock shatters the ML record by stealing 118 bases.

- Minnesota's Rod Carew takes the AL bat crown (.364) and leads in hits (218).

Hank Aaron

- White Sox Dick Allen tops the AL in homers (32) and SA (.563).

- Ron LeFlore debuts with the Tigers a year after being released from prison.

- Oakland's Catfish Hunter wins the AL Cy Young in a close vote over Ranger Ferguson Jenkins, as both tie for the ML lead in wins with 25.

- LA's Mike Marshall appears in an all-time ML-record 106 games and is the first reliever to cop the Cy Young Award.

- The Reds' Pete Rose makes an ML-record 771 plate appearances. Rose tops the ML with 110 runs and 45 doubles.

- On June 4 in Cleveland, 10-cent beer night results in a near riot and the forfeit of the game to Texas.

- Brewer Don Money's .989 fielding average sets an ML season record for a third baseman.

- The Orioles set an AL record when they win five straight games by shutouts.

- Cincinnati's Johnny Bench leads the NL with 129 RBI and 315 total bases.

- Atlanta's Ralph Garr tops the NL with a .353 BA, 214 hits, and 17 triples.

- The NL wins the All-Star Game 7-2 at Pittsburgh for its 11th win in the last 12 games.

- Ray Kroc, founder of McDonald's, buys the Padres.

- The Cards beat the Mets 4-3 on September 11 in a 25-inning night game.

- Detroit's Al Kaline gets his 3,000th hit, then retires after the season. He misses becoming the first AL player to register 3,000 hits and 400 home runs by one round-tripper.

- George Steinbrenner is suspended by Commissioner Bowie Kuhn for a year because of his part in the Watergate scandal.

- Buzz Capra of the Braves tops the ML in ERA (2.28).

- Ron Hunt leads the NL in being hit by pitches a record seventh consecutive season.

- The Orioles and Yankees battle it out in an exciting AL East stretch run. Baltimore wins 27 of its last 33 games (15 by one run) to edge New York by two. The O's are no match for the A's in the ALCS, falling in four games.

- The Pirates and Dodgers take their respective NL divisions. LA wins the NLCS in four.

- Oakland, under first-year manager Alvin Dark, becomes the last team to win the World Series three years in a row. Four of the five games are decided by 3-2 scores.

Lynn pulls off unprecedented double... Robinson breaks managerial color line... Reds prevail in Series classic

- Boston's Fred Lynn becomes the only player in ML history to be named Rookie of the Year and MVP in the same season. Lynn tops the AL in runs (103), doubles (47), runs produced (187), and SA (.566). He drives in 105 runs, while rookie teammate Jim Rice knocks in 102.

- Cincinnati's Joe Morgan wins the NL MVP Award.

- The Mets' Tom Seaver leads the NL with 22 wins and cops his third Cy Young Award.

- Baltimore's Jim Palmer wins his second AL Cy Young, as he leads the loop in ERA (2.09) and shutouts (10) and ties for the lead in wins (23).

- In a historic decision, arbitrator Peter Seitz grants pitchers Dave McNally and Andy Messersmith free agency.

- Chicago's Bill Madlock takes his first NL bat crown (.354).

- Frank Robinson is named manager of Cleveland to become the first African-American skipper in major-league history.

- Nolan Ryan throws his fourth no-hitter in three years on June 1 vs. Baltimore.

- The Tigers lose 19 games in a row.

- Yankee Catfish Hunter becomes the last ML pitcher to toss 30 complete games.

- Davey Lopes of LA sets an ML record when he steals 38 consecutive bases without being caught.

- The Pirates beat the Cubs 22-0 on September 16—the most one-sided shutout in the majors since 1883. In the game, Rennie Stennett of the Pirates becomes the lone player in the 20th century to go 7-for-7 in a nine-inning game.

- Four A's pitchers combine to no-hit California on September 28.

- Bob Watson of the Astros scores the millionth run in ML history.

- Dave Cash of the Phils sets an ML record with 699 at-bats.

- Cincinnati's Pete Rose leads the NL in runs (112) and doubles (47).

- Phillie Mike Schmidt paces the majors with 38 homers.

- Brewer George Scott leads the AL in RBI (109) and total bases (318) and ties Oakland's Reggie Jackson for the lead in homers (36).

- Billy Martin is fired as Texas manager in midseason, then hired by the Yankees to replace Bill Virdon.

- Casey Stengel dies.

- Ted Simmons of the Cardinals sets a big-league record for catchers with 193 hits.

- Boston surprises Baltimore to win the AL East, then ends Oakland's three-year stretch of dominance with a sweep of the ALCS. The Red Sox outscore the A's 18-7 in the three-game whitewashing.

- Cincinnati's Big Red Machine runs away with the West title before sweeping the Pirates in the LCS. It is Pittsburgh's fourth NLCS loss in six years.

- The Reds and Red Sox put on a World Series that ranks among the most memorable ever played. Carlton Fisk's dramatic, 12th-inning home run in the sixth game at Fenway Park stays just fair for a 7-6 Boston win, forcing a seventh game.

◊ Cincinnati rallies from a 3-0 deficit in the finale for a 4-3 victory and the title. Morgan's soft, two-out single in the top of the ninth inning drives in the winning run.

Carlton Fisk, World Series home run

1976

Big Red Machine defends crown... Brett claims controversial bat title... Aaron retires with 755 homers

- Cincinnati's Joe Morgan is again voted the NL MVP, after stealing 60 bases and leading in SA (.576).

- Thurman Munson is named AL MVP. He tops Yankee hitters in the World Series with a .529 BA.

- San Diego's Randy Jones takes the NL Cy Young, topping the loop with 22 wins.

- Baltimore's Jim Palmer claims his third AL Cy Young in four years, as he leads the league with 22 wins.

- In June, A's owner Charles O. Finley tries to sell Joe Rudi, Rollie Fingers, and Vida Blue, but Commissioner Bowie Kuhn vetoes the deals.

- The Royals' George Brett wins a controversial bat crown over teammate Hal McRae, .333 to .332.

Brett wins the title on his last at-bat of the season, as Twins outfielder Steve Braun seems to deliberately misplay the ball. Brett leads the AL in hits (215), total bases (298), and triples (14).

- Philly's Mike Schmidt leads the majors in homers (38) and total bases (306). Schmidt hits four homers in a 10-inning game on April 17.

- The NL wins the All-Star Game 7-1 at Philadelphia, as Detroit rookie Mark Fidrych starts for the AL and takes the loss.

> **"I came to the Braves on business, and I intended to see that business was good as long as I could."**
>
> —*Hank Aaron*

- Fidrych is named AL Rookie of the Year. He wins 19 games and leads the AL in ERA (2.34) and complete games (24).

- Hank Aaron retires with all-time ML records for homers (755), RBI (2,297), and total bases (6,856).

- The only "rainout" in Astrodome history occurs on June 15 when heavy rains prevent fans and umps from getting to the dome.

- Ted Turner buys the Braves.

- On September 12, at age 54, Minnie Minoso of the White Sox becomes the oldest player to get a hit in an ML game.

- The Reds' Pete Rose tops the NL in hits (215), doubles (42), and runs (130).

- Chicago's Bill Madlock wins the NL bat crown (.339).

- The National League celebrates its 100th year.

- California's Nolan Ryan totes a 17-18 record, with eight shutout losses and a league-leading seven shutout wins.

- After the season, Tom Lasorda is named to succeed Walter Alston as LA manager.

- The *Bad News Bears* plays in movie theaters.

- Detroit's Ron LeFlore hits safely in 30 consecutive games.

- Cincinnati dominates the NL, leading by a wide margin in most offensive categories en route to 102 victories. The Phillies beat the Pirates by nine games in the NL East but are no match for the Reds in a three-game NLCS sweep.

- The Yankees win their first AL pennant since 1964, a long drought for the most storied franchise in the game. They win the AL East by a double-digit margin over Baltimore and cop the ALCS in five games over the Royals. A Chris Chambliss homer wins the finale in the ninth.

> Dan Driessen of the Reds becomes the first NL designated hitter when he comes to the plate in the second inning of the World Series opener.

- The Big Red Machine blows out New York in one of the most lopsided World Series to date. The Reds outscore the Yankees 22-8, with the lone competitive game a 4-3 decision.

- The Reds' Johnny Bench leads all World Series hitters with a .533 BA, two homers, and six RBI. George Foster bats .429 for the winners.

- Free-agency bidding begins in earnest after the 1976 season. The Yankees sign Reggie Jackson for $3.5 million.

*"Mr. October" powers the Yankees...
Carew makes a run at .400...AL gets
northern exposure*

- The AL swells to 14 teams, adding the Toronto Blue Jays and Seattle Mariners.

- Olympic Stadium in Montreal hosts its first baseball game—Phils vs. Expos.

- Cincinnati's George Foster is named NL MVP, as he leads the ML with 52 homers and 149 RBI. Foster also leads the NL in runs (124), SA (.631), total bases (388), and runs produced (221).

- Minnesota's Rod Carew wins the AL MVP Award after hitting .388, the top BA in the majors since expansion. Carew leads the ML with 239 hits, 128 runs, and a .452 OBP and the AL in triples (16) and runs produced (214).

- Philadelphia's Steve Carlton wins the Cy Young Award in the NL, as he leads the majors with 23 wins.

- Yankee Sparky Lyle becomes the first reliever to win the AL Cy Young.

- California's Nolan Ryan fans an ML-high 341 batters in 299 innings.

- Boston's Jim Rice leads the AL in homers (39), SA (.593), and total bases (382).

- The Dodgers become the first team in history with four 30-homer men—Ron Cey, Steve Garvey, Dusty Baker, and Reggie Smith.

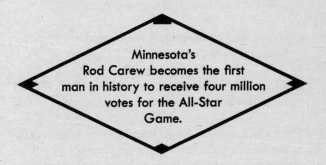

Minnesota's Rod Carew becomes the first man in history to receive four million votes for the All-Star Game.

- On April 10, Cleveland and Boston combine to score an ML-record 19 runs in one inning.

- Chicago's Chet Lemon sets the AL record for outfielders with 512 putouts.

- The Royals put together a 16-game win streak.

- The Mets, frustrated by salary disputes with Tom Seaver, trade him to the Reds for four players of no particular consequence.

- On July 4, the Red Sox beat Toronto 9-6 on the strength of eight homers.

- KC's Hal McRae leads the ML with 54 doubles.

- Pittsburgh's Dave Parker tops the NL in BA (.338), hits (215), and doubles (44).

- Pirate John Candelaria leads the majors with a 2.34 ERA and an .800 winning pct.

- Duane Kuiper of the Indians homers for the only time in a career that spans 3,379 at-bats.

- AL teams combine to score more than 10,000 runs, the first time that mark is achieved.

- Brooks Robinson retires holding several career fielding marks, including top fielding average by a third baseman and most games played at that position. His 23-year career is spent solely with the Orioles.

- Detroit's Mark Fidrych injures his knee in a spring-training game. It alters his delivery and he is never again the pitcher he was in his rookie year.

- The Royals are the first expansion team in the 20th century to top the majors in wins, as they net 102.

- Kansas City's World Series aspirations are dashed by the 100-win Yankees in a five-game ALCS. New York rallies for three runs in the ninth inning to win the deciding game 5-3.

- The heavy-hitting Dodgers win the NL West by 10 games and encounter little trouble from the Phillies in the NLCS. LA wins in four, with Baker slugging two key home runs.

> **"I don't want to be a hero. I don't want to be a star. It just works out that way."**
>
> —*Reggie Jackson*

- The Yankees win their first World Series title since 1962. It takes six games and includes two pitching victories from Mike Torrez.

- Reggie Jackson, "Mr. October," leads World Series hitters with a .450 BA and five homers, including three in Game 6 on three consecutive pitches.

- The Yankees' Billy Martin wins his only world championship as a manager.

1978

Steinbrenner forces Martin out ... Rose hits in 44 straight ... Yanks again leave Dodgers blue

- Yankee Ron Guidry goes 25-3, sets the winning pct. record for a 25-game winner at .893, and tops the ML with a 1.74 ERA. Guidry is a unanimous choice for the AL Cy Young Award.

- Padre Gaylord Perry wins the NL Cy Young, becoming the first hurler to win the award in both leagues.

- Boston's Jim Rice edges out Guidry for the AL MVP Award. Rice leads the AL in hits (213), home runs (46), RBI (139), triples (15), total bases (406), SA (.600), and runs produced (214).

- Minnesota's Rod Carew takes his second consecutive AL bat crown (.333).

- Texas's Bobby Bonds is a member of the 30-30 club (30 homers, 30 steals) for an ML-record fifth time.

- Pirate Dave Parker is named NL MVP. Parker repeats as NL bat champ (.334) and also leads the loop in total bases (340), SA (.585), and runs produced (189).

- Billy Martin resigns as Yankee manager in midseason under pressure from owner George Steinbrenner. New manager Bob Lemon leads the Yanks to the flag.

- The Reds' Pete Rose sets a modern NL record by hitting in 44 consecutive games; his streak ends in Atlanta on August 1. Rose gets his 3,000th hit, making him the first switch-hitter to do so.

> **"When I was a little boy, I wanted to be a baseball player and join the circus. With the Yankees, I've accomplished both."**
>
> —Graig Nettles

- Cincinnati's George Foster again tops the NL in homers (40) and RBI (120).

- California's Lyman Bostock, the AL bat crown runner-up in 1977, is shot to death.

- The Dodgers are the first team to draw more than three million fans in a season.

- The Reds' Joe Morgan's ML-record skein of 91 consecutive errorless games ends.

- The NL wins the All-Star Game 7-3 at San Diego for its seventh consecutive victory.

- On July 30, the Braves suffer the worst loss by a home team in NL history, as they're blown out by the Expos 19-0.

- The Giants get Vida Blue from the A's for seven players and $390,000.

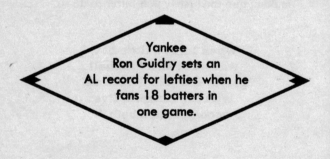

Yankee Ron Guidry sets an AL record for lefties when he fans 18 batters in one game.

- Boston third baseman Butch Hobson becomes the first big-league regular in 62 years to post a fielding percentage below .900.

- Detroit's Ron LeFlore tops the AL in steals (68) and runs (126).

- Cardinal Keith Hernandez wins his first of an ML-record 11 consecutive Gold Gloves at first base.

- San Diego's Rollie Fingers leads the majors with 37 saves.

- The Pirates' Kent Tekulve leads the majors with 91 appearances and notches 31 saves.

- The Red Sox blow a 14-game lead over the Yankees. New York delivers its lethal blow in a four-game September series at Fenway Park, winning by scores of 15-3, 13-2, 7-0, and 7-4 in what becomes known as the "Boston Massacre." New York then defeats Boston in a playoff 5-4, thanks to a home run by Bucky Dent.

- The Yankees go on to beat the Royals for the third straight year in the ALCS. This time just four games are needed.

- The Phillies lose in the NLCS for the third year in a row, as LA's Steve Garvey rips four home runs in as many games. LA thus defends its NL pennant, setting up the first World Series rematch since 1958.

- New York wins its second consecutive Series title. Dent bats .417 with seven RBI to win MVP accolades. Third baseman Graig Nettles makes several brilliant defensive plays.

1979

"Pops" has Pirates dancing... Plane crash takes Munson's life... Yaz, Brock stroke No. 3,000

- Pirate Willie Stargell, age 39, becomes the oldest MVP in history, as he and Cardinal Keith Hernandez finish in a tie for the NL award.

- Hernandez tops the NL in batting (.344), doubles (48), runs (116), runs produced (210), and OBP (.421).

- Angel Don Baylor wins the AL MVP Award after leading the ML in runs (120), RBI (139), and runs produced (223).

- Boston's Fred Lynn wins the AL bat crown (.333) and also leads in SA (.637).

- Baltimore's Mike Flanagan leads the ML in wins with 23 and cops the AL Cy Young Award.

- Cubs reliever Bruce Sutter wins the NL Cy Young, as he paces the majors with 37 saves.

- Cub Dave Kingman tops the ML in homers (48) and NL in SA (.613).

- San Diego's Dave Winfield tops the NL in RBI (118) and total bases (333).

- Major-league attendance soars to a record 34 million.

- The average player's salary shoots up to $113,500.

- Yankee star Thurman Munson dies in a plane crash on August 2.

- Phillie Larry Bowa sets an ML record for shortstops with a .991 fielding average.

- Toronto loses 109 games.

- Pete Rose, no longer with the Reds after joining the Phillies as a free agent, gets 200 or more hits for an ML-record 10th time.

- Phil Niekro of Atlanta and his brother Joe Niekro of Houston tie for the NL lead in wins (21).

- Billy Martin takes over for Bob Lemon as Yankee skipper 65 games into the season, only to be fired again after the campaign.

- Milwaukee's Gorman Thomas leads the AL with 45 homers. He also has 123 RBI.

- Cardinal Lou Brock gets his 3,000th hit. Brock retires with the ML record for career stolen bases (938).

- Boston's Carl Yastrzemski gets his 3,000th hit.

- Cardinal Garry Templeton is the first switch-hitter to get at least 100 hits from each side of the plate in a season.

- On May 31, Detroit's Pat Underwood makes his ML debut against brother Tom of Toronto. Pat beats Tom 1-0.

Willie Stargell

- The Twins send Rod Carew to the Angels for four players.

- Royal Darrell Porter becomes the first catcher since Mickey Cochrane in 1933 to lead the AL in OBP (.429) and sets a league record for walks by a catcher (121).

- Houston's J.R. Richard leads the ML in Ks (313) and ERA (2.71).

- After the 1979 season, the Astros sign free agent Nolan Ryan for an estimated $1 million a year.

- Dancing to the theme song "We Are Family" and riding the bat of Stargell, Pittsburgh edges Montreal by two games in the NL East and sweeps the Reds in the NLCS. Two of the three games go to extra innings.

- The Angels win their first division crown, beating out the Twins by six games in the AL West. The California magic ends in the ALCS when the Orioles prevail in four games. The first three games go down to the wire before an 8-0 Baltimore win wraps it up.

- The Pirates overcome a 3-1 deficit to win the Series title. Stargell's two-run homer in the sixth inning puts Pittsburgh ahead for good in the decisive 4-1 win. Five Pirates have 10 or more hits in the Series, and Tekulve saves three games.

Brett falls 10 points short of .400...Mota comes through in a pinch...Phillies end championship drought

- KC's George Brett is named AL MVP, as he hits .390 after flirting with .400 for much of the season.

- Phillie Mike Schmidt sets an ML record for third basemen with 48 home runs. He leads the ML in homers, RBI (121), SA (.624), and total bases (342) and grabs NL MVP honors.

- Oriole Steve Stone wins the AL Cy Young Award, as he leads the ML with 25 wins.

- Philly's Steve Carlton cops the NL Cy Young, as he wins 24 games.

- On October 5, LA's Manny Mota collects his ML-record 150th career pinch hit.

- Houston pitching star J.R. Richard's career is ended by a stroke.

- Mike Parrott of Seattle loses 16 straight games.

- Cub relief ace Bruce Sutter is awarded a staggering salary of $700,000 when he takes the club to arbitration.

- After losing to the Royals in the ALCS, Yankee manager Dick Howser is fired despite leading the club to 103 wins during the regular season.

- Padre Ozzie Smith sets an ML record for shortstops with 621 assists.

- The NL wins the All-Star Game 4-2 at LA. It's the league's ninth straight victory and 17th triumph in its last 18 games.

- Willie Wilson of the Royals sets an ML record with 705 at-bats. Wilson leads the AL in hits (230) and runs (133) and ties for the lead in triples (15).

- Income from TV accounts for a record 30 percent of the game's $500 million in revenues.

- The average player now makes about $185,000.

- KC is the first AL expansion team to win a pennant.

- In their first year under Billy Martin, the A's rise to second in the AL West and post 94 complete games, most in the majors since 1946.

George Brett

- Cub Bill Buckner leads the NL in batting at .324.

- Cardinal Keith Hernandez tops the NL in runs (111), runs produced (194), and OBP (.410).

- Brewer Cecil Cooper leads the AL in RBI (122) and total bases (335).

- New York's Reggie Jackson and Milwaukee's Ben Oglivie tie for the AL homer lead (41).

- Oakland's Rickey Henderson becomes the first AL player to steal 100 bases (100).

- On September 10, Montreal's Bill Gullickson sets a rookie record when he strikes out 18 in a game.

- Dallas Green's Phillies clinch the NL East in the penultimate game of the season, as Schmidt's two-run homer in the top of the 11th inning beats the Expos.

- The NLCS pits the Phillies and Astros in what turns out to be a five-game classic. The final four games go into extra innings. The Astros win Game 3 in 11 for a 2-1 series lead, but the Phillies take the final pair. In Game 5, Philly overcomes a three-run deficit in the eighth and wins in the 10th when Garry Maddox's double plates Del Unser.

- Kansas City wins its first AL pennant, running away with the AL West and avenging three straight ALCS losses to the Yankees with a three-game sweep.

- A six-game World Series sees the Phillies claim their first world championship. Carlton becomes the first NL starting pitcher to win two Series games since Steve Blass in 1971. Tug McGraw gets two saves. Schmidt bats .381.

Baseball strikes out, Reds lose out... Rose sets NL hit record...Dodgers avenge Series setbacks

- A players strike cancels eight weeks of the season. The settlement results in the first split-season campaign in the majors since 1892. Owing to the split-season format, the team with baseball's best record, Cincinnati, doesn't qualify for postseason play.

- LA's Fernando Valenzuela wins NL Rookie of the Year and Cy Young honors, as he tops the NL in innings (192), complete games (11), shutouts (eight), and Ks (180).

- Milwaukee's Rollie Fingers is named MVP and Cy Young winner in the AL. He leads the majors with 28 saves.

- Philly's Pete Rose tops the ML in hits (140) to become the only 40-year-old player ever to accomplish the feat. Rose collects his 3,631st hit, breaking Stan Musial's NL record.

- Phillie Mike Schmidt is the NL MVP. Schmidt paces the ML in homers (31), RBI (91), total bases (228), SA (.644), runs produced (138), and OBP (.439). He also leads the NL in walks (73) and runs (78).

- Phillie Steve Carlton becomes the first ML left-hander to collect 3,000 career strikeouts.

- On August 24, Kent Hrbek of the Twins homers in his first ML game. On September 20, two other Minnesota rookies, Gary Gaetti and Tim Laudner, also connect for four-baggers in their first major-league contests.

> **"All last year we tried to teach him English, and the only word he learned was 'million.'"**
>
> —LA manager Tommy Lasorda on Fernando Valenzuela

- The NL wins its 10th straight All-Star Game, 5-4 in Cleveland. Vida Blue of the Giants becomes the first pitcher to win the midsummer classic for both leagues.

- Houston's Nolan Ryan throws an ML-record fifth no-hitter on September 26 vs. LA. Ryan has the best ERA in the majors (1.69).

- Charles Finley sells the A's to Levi's jeans magnates.

- Bill Veeck sells the White Sox for the second time in his life.

- The Cubs are sold to the Chicago Tribune Company.

- Len Barker of Cleveland pitches a perfect game against Toronto on May 15.

- Rochester and Pawtucket of the International League play a 33-inning game—longest in organized-baseball history—over a two-day period.

- Expo Tim Raines sets an ML rookie record with 71 steals despite an abbreviated season.

- Boston's Carney Lansford wins the AL bat crown at .336.

- Pirate Bill Madlock barely qualifies for the NL BA title but wins at .341.

- Oakland's Rickey Henderson leads the AL in runs (89) and steals (56).

- Three of the four Division Series go the five-game distance—Expos over Phillies in the NL East, Dodgers over Astros in the NL West, and Yankees over Brewers in the AL East. The A's sweep a 50-53 Royals team to win the AL West.

- The Dodgers extend their nail-biting postseason with a five-game win over the Expos in the NLCS. Rick Monday breaks a 1-1 tie with a two-out home run off Steve Rogers in the ninth inning of the finale, giving LA a 2-1 victory.

- The Yankees outscore the A's 20-4 in a three-game ALCS sweep.

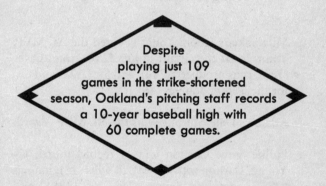

Despite playing just 109 games in the strike-shortened season, Oakland's pitching staff records a 10-year baseball high with 60 complete games.

- New York keeps its postseason momentum by winning the first two Series games, then runs out of steam in a hurry. The Dodgers take the next four, wrapping up their first world title since 1965 and atoning for their poor Series luck against the Yanks. Steve Garvey hits .417.

- Yankee relief pitcher George Frazier is tagged with three consecutive Series losses, a new record.

Henderson swipes stolen base record... Carlton wins fourth Cy Young... Cardinals fly high

- Milwaukee's Robin Yount is voted the AL MVP. Yount leads the circuit in hits (210), total bases (367), runs produced (214), and SA (.578) and ties for the lead in doubles (46).

- Atlanta's Dale Murphy wins the NL MVP Award.

- Phillie Steve Carlton wins a record fourth Cy Young. Carlton tops the ML in wins (23), innings (296), complete games (19), Ks (286), and shutouts (six).

- Milwaukee's Pete Vuckovich wins a controversial Cy Young vote in the AL.

- The Braves open the season with 13 consecutive wins, an NL record.

- Oakland's Rickey Henderson steals an ML-record 130 bases.

- Carl Yastrzemski retires after 23 years with the Red Sox, tying Brooks Robinson's record for most seasons with the same team.

- Milwaukee's Rollie Fingers becomes the first in history to collect 300 saves.

- The NL wins its 11th straight All-Star Game, 4-1 at Montreal.

- Phillie Garry Maddox wins his last of eight consecutive Gold Gloves as an NL outfielder.

> **"He's like a little kid in a train station. You turn your back on him and he's gone."**
>
> —*Doc Medich on Rickey Henderson*

- Joel Youngblood gets hits for two different teams in two different cities in the same day when he's traded from the Mets to the Expos.

- The Metrodome opens on April 6, the Mariners vs. Twins.

- Royal Hal McRae tops the majors with 133 RBI, a record for a DH.

- Seattle's Gaylord Perry wins his 300th game on May 6.

- Royal John Wathan sets an ML record for catchers with 36 stolen bases.

- Montreal's Al Oliver leads the NL in BA (.331), hits (204), doubles (43), and total bases (317) and ties for the lead in RBI (109).

- Philadelphia's Mike Schmidt leads the NL in walks (107), OBP (.407), and SA (.547).

- KC's Willie Wilson tops the AL in batting (.332).

- New York's Dave Kingman leads the NL with 37 homers. His .204 BA is the lowest ever for a homer leader.

- Angel Reggie Jackson and the Brewers' Gorman Thomas tie for the AL homer lead with 39.

- Boston's Bob Stanley sets an AL record by pitching 168 innings in relief.

- Terry Felton leaves baseball with an 0-16 lifetime record—worst mark ever.

- For the first time in history, the Yankees' home opener is canceled by a blizzard.

- The Braves make the playoffs for the first time since 1969 but fall to the Cards in a three-game NLCS. St. Louis edges the Phillies in the NL East and wins its first pennant since 1968.

- Milwaukee wins the AL East on the last day of the season after Baltimore closes a four-game gap with three straight wins over the Brewers. California beats the Royals by three games in the AL West.

- The Angels become the first team to take the first two games of an LCS but fail to reach the World Series. The Brewers come back with 5-3, 9-5, and 4-3 victories, as Cecil Cooper's seventh-inning single breaks a tie in the finale.

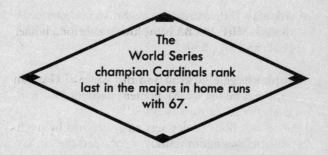

The World Series champion Cardinals rank last in the majors in home runs with 67.

- Brewer Paul Molitor gets a World Series-record five hits in the opener, a 10-0 Milwaukee rout. The Cardinals win the next two games, then fall twice more to the Brewers before sweeping the final two contests for the Series title.

- George Hendrick and Lonnie Smith lead the Cardinals with .321 Series averages. Joaquin Andujar goes 2-0 with a 1.35 ERA. The Brewers' Molitor bats .414.

1983

White Sox win ugly... Ryan, Carlton pass strikeout king... Orioles treat Altobelli to world title

- Atlanta's Dale Murphy wins his second consecutive NL MVP Award. Murphy leads the NL in RBI (121) and SA (.540).

- Baltimore's Cal Ripken is named AL MVP. Ripken tops the ML in hits (211) and doubles (47) and leads the AL in runs (121).

- Philadelphia's John Denny is awarded the NL Cy Young after topping the loop with 19 wins.

- LaMarr Hoyt of Chicago wins the AL Cy Young and leads the ML in wins (24).

- Padre Steve Garvey's NL-record streak of 1,207 consecutive games ends when he breaks his thumb.

- Houston's Nolan Ryan and Philly's Steve Carlton both surpass Walter Johnson's career K record of 3,508.

- KC's Dan Quisenberry sets an ML record with 45 saves.

- Boston's Jim Rice leads the AL in homers (39) and total bases (344) and ties for the lead in RBI (126).

- Boston's Wade Boggs wins his first AL bat crown (.361).

- Pittsburgh's Bill Madlock wins his fourth and final bat crown in the NL (.323).

- With 108 steals, Oakland's Rickey Henderson becomes the first to swipe at least 100 bases in consecutive years.

"I found a delivery in my flaw."

—KC's Dan Quisenberry, appraising his unorthodox pitching style

- The Louisville Red Birds become the first team in minor-league history to draw one million fans in a season.

- KC's George Brett hits his famous "pine tar" homer versus the Yankees on July 24.

- On July 3, Texas beats the A's with 12 runs in the 15th inning—an ML record for most runs scored in an overtime frame.

- The AL breaks its skein of 11 consecutive losses in the All-Star Game by beating the NL 13-3 at Comiskey Park. California's Fred Lynn hits a grand slam.

- Seattle is the first ML team in the 20th century to go through a season without playing a doubleheader.

- Dodger Steve Howe and Royal Willie Aikens are the first players to be suspended for a full year for drug abuse.

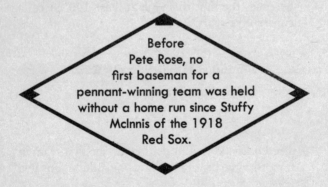

Before Pete Rose, no first baseman for a pennant-winning team was held without a home run since Stuffy McInnis of the 1918 Red Sox.

- Expo Tim Raines sets an NL record when he scores 19.6 percent of his team's runs, as he leads the ML with 133 runs.

- Phillie Mike Schmidt tops the NL in homers (40), walks (128), and OBP (.402).

- Atlee Hammaker of the Giants paces the majors with a 2.25 ERA.

- Met Rusty Staub sets an ML record with 81 at-bats as a pinch hitter.

- "Winning ugly," according to manager Tony LaRussa, the White Sox capture 99 games and the AL West title. Four players hit at least 20 home runs.

- Joe Altobelli replaces the legendary Earl Weaver as skipper of the Orioles, and his team wins a pennant for him. Baltimore then knocks out Chicago in four games in the ALCS.

- The aging Phillies have enough mileage to win the NL East, then beat the West champion Dodgers in four NLCS games. Pete Rose, at age 42, becomes the oldest Series regular ever.

- Baltimore concludes its impressive run to the World Series title with a five-game win over the Phils. The Orioles get one win each from four different pitchers while holding Philly to a .195 team average and 1.8 runs per game.

- Rick Dempsey bats .385 and is named Series MVP. Rose hits .313 in a losing cause.

1984

Ueberroth takes baseball's top seat...Sandberg tears up the NL...Tigers start 35-5, roar to title

- Tiger reliever Willie Hernandez claims Cy Young and MVP honors, as he earns 32 saves in his first 32 save opportunities.

- Chicago's Ryne Sandberg takes the NL MVP Award. Sandberg leads the NL in runs (114) and ties for the lead in runs produced (179) and triples (19).

- Cub Rick Sutcliffe becomes the only Cy Young winner who began the year with another team. He goes 4-5 with Cleveland, is traded, and then goes 16-1 with the Cubs.

- Met Dwight Gooden is named NL Rookie of the Year, as he sets an ML rookie K record with 276.

- The Tigers win 26 of their first 30 games, and 35 of their first 40—best starts for any ML team in the 20th century. They also win an AL-record 17 straight games on the road.

- Tony Armas of Boston leads the ML in homers (43), RBI (123), and total bases (339).

- Montreal's Pete Rose gets his 4,000th hit on April 21. Rose achieves 100 or more hits for the 22nd consecutive year, an ML record. He also sets an ML record when he plays in his 3,309th game.

- California's Reggie Jackson hits his 500th homer on September 17.

- Cardinal Bruce Sutter ties an ML record with 45 saves.

- Atlanta's Dale Murphy leads the NL in total bases (332) and SA (.547).

- Boston's Dwight Evans tops the ML in runs (121) and runs produced (193).

- Yankee Don Mattingly leads the AL in BA (.343), hits (207), and doubles (44).

- Phillie Steve Carlton wins his 300th game.

- Mike Witt of the Angels pitches a perfect game against Texas on September 30, the final day of the season.

- Padre Tony Gwynn wins his first NL bat crown with a .351 average, and he tops the ML with 213 hits.

Ryne Sandberg

- After the regular season, Peter Ueberroth replaces Bowie Kuhn as commissioner.

- Philly's Mike Schmidt ties Murphy for the NL homer title (36) and Montreal's Gary Carter for the RBI crown (106).

- Dick Williams ties Bill McKechnie's record by taking his third different team, the Padres, to a pennant.

- Houston's Dickie Thon is beaned, suffers damaged vision, and will never regain his hitting ability.

- Joe Morgan's 265th home run breaks Rogers Hornsby's career mark for second basemen.

- Jim Frey leads the Cubs to a division title in his first season, just as he did earlier in KC.

- Long-suffering Cubs fans believe this is finally the year for a return to the Series when the North Siders win the NL East and take the first two LCS games from the Padres. San Diego, the first second-wave expansion team to win an NL flag, takes the final three games.

- The Tigers prove their hot start is no fluke, sweeping the Royals in the ALCS and winning a five-game Series over San Diego. Kirk Gibson socks two homers in Game 5 to clinch it. Alan Trammell bats .450 with two homers and six RBI. Jack Morris wins two complete games.

- Detroit's Sparky Anderson becomes the first manager to win world championships in both leagues.

- Including the postseason, the Tigers post a 100-0 record when leading after eight innings.

*Rose becomes the all-time hit king...
Denkinger riles Cards...Saberhagen,
comeback Royals win Series*

- Willie McGee of the Cards is voted NL MVP, as he leads the league in BA (.353), hits (216), and triples (18).

- New York's Don Mattingly is named AL MVP. His 145 RBI lead the ML by 20. Mattingly also leads the AL in runs produced (217), total bases (370), and doubles (48).

- The Mets' Dwight Gooden wins the NL Cy Young Award, as he leads the NL in wins (24), ERA (1.53), Ks (268), complete games (16), and innings (277).

- Kansas City's Bret Saberhagen cops AL Cy Young honors.

- Boston's Wade Boggs leads the majors with 240 hits, most in the majors since 1930. Boggs also leads the ML in BA (.368) and OBP (.452).

- Vince Coleman of the Cards steals 110 bases, setting an ML rookie record.

- Yankee Rickey Henderson scores 146 runs, most in the majors since 1949.

- On September 11, Pete Rose cracks his 4,192nd career hit, breaking Ty Cobb's ML record.

Pete Rose after breaking Ty Cobb's hit record

- Baltimore's Cal Ripken breaks Buck Freeman's record for consecutive innings played, as he reaches 5,342 innings without respite.

- Don Sutton becomes the first pitcher in ML history to fan 100 or more hitters in 20 consecutive seasons.

- Padre Steve Garvey's ML-record streak of 193 consecutive errorless games at first base ends.

- Angel Bobby Grich's .997 fielding average sets an ML record for second basemen.

- Larry Bowa retires with the record for highest career fielding average by a shortstop (.980).

- Houston's Nolan Ryan fans his 4,000th batter on July 11.

- The Angels' Rod Carew collects his 3,000th hit.

- Yankee Phil Niekro picks up his 300th win.

- Tom Seaver of the White Sox collects win No. 300.

- Darrell Evans is the first to notch 40 or more homers in a season in each league, as he cracks an ML-leading 40 for Detroit.

- The players strike on August 6 for two days.

- Atlanta's Dale Murphy leads the NL in homers (37), runs (118), and walks (90).

- Dave Parker, now with the Reds, tops the NL in RBI (125), total bases (350), and doubles (42).

- Toronto edges New York by two games in the AL East.

- The LCS format is expanded to a best-of-seven series, to the delight of KC. The Royals win the final three games after falling behind the Blue Jays three games to one.

- The Cardinals nip the Mets in the NL East, then outlast the Dodgers in six games for their second flag of the 1980s. Ozzie Smith wins the final game of the LCS with a left-handed home run, the first of his career from that side.

- The Royals, trailing three games to two, get a World Series lift when umpire Don Denkinger rules Jorge Orta safe at first base in the bottom of the ninth inning in Game 6. Replays show the KC pinch hitter was out. The Royals turn the break into a two-run rally to win the game 2-1.

- Saberhagen blanks the Cards in the finale, 11-0, as the Royals win their first Series crown. It is the second win for Saberhagen. George Brett leads the KC offense with 10 Series hits.

1986

Rocket Roger strikes out 20 ... Schmidt wins record eighth HR title ... Mets stage Series rally

- Boston's Roger Clemens wins the AL Cy Young and MVP Awards, as he leads the ML in wins (24) and winning pct. (.857). Clemens fans an all-time ML-record 20 Mariners on April 29.

- Philadelphia's Mike Schmidt is named NL MVP and sets an NL record by leading his league in homers for the eighth time, as he clubs 37. Schmidt leads the NL in SA (.547) and RBI (119) and also wins the last of his 10 Gold Gloves, an NL record for third basemen.

- Houston's Mike Scott wins the NL Cy Young. He no-hits the Giants on September 25—the only no-hitter in NL history to clinch a pennant or division crown.

- Oakland's Jose Canseco is named AL Rookie of the Year, as he hammers 33 homers and totals 117 RBI.

- For the first time in history, every club in the majors exceeds one million in attendance.

- Don Mattingly hits .352 and sets Yankees franchise records with 238 hits and 53 doubles. Mattingly tops the ML in hits, doubles, SA (.573), and total bases (388).

- Boston's Wade Boggs leads the ML in BA (.357), walks (105), and OBP (.455).

- Pete Rose retires holding ML career records for hits (4,256), games (3,562), and at-bats (14,053).

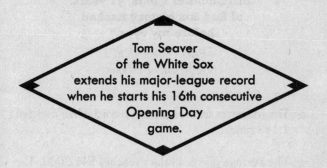

Tom Seaver of the White Sox extends his major-league record when he starts his 16th consecutive Opening Day game.

- Cardinal Todd Worrell is named NL Rookie of the Year, as he sets an ML rookie record with 36 saves.

- KC's Bo Jackson becomes the second Heisman Trophy winner to play in the majors.

- On July 6, Atlanta's Bob Horner becomes the only player in the 20th century to hit four homers in a game lost by his team.

- Yankee Dave Righetti sets an ML record with 46 saves.

- Phillie Steve Carlton becomes the first lefty to collect 4,000 career Ks.

- California's Don Sutton wins his 300th game.

> **"When the ball went through Bill Buckner's legs, 41 years of Red Sox history flashed before my eyes."**
>
> —Peter Gammons in a Boston Globe column

- The Mariners set an AL team record when they fan 1,148 times.

- The average player's salary reaches $412,000. The minimum salary is now $62,500.

- Minnesota's Bert Blyleven gives up 50 home runs, setting an ML record.

- Toronto's Jesse Barfield leads the majors with 40 homers.

- Hank Greenberg dies on September 4.

- The Mets whip the rest of the NL East by 21½ games, the largest margin in the majors since the start of divisional play.

- Houston wins the NL West, then gives New York a battle in the LCS before falling in six games. The Mets win the clincher 7-6 in 16 innings after rallying for three runs in the ninth to force extra frames.

- The Red Sox clinch the AL East in the season's final week, then play it even closer in the LCS against California. Trailing three games to one, Boston claims the final three for its first flag since 1975. Dave Henderson's two-out, two-strike, two-run homer in the ninth inning of Game 5 keeps the Sox alive.

- Boston appears ready to clinch the World Series in Game 6 with a 5-3 lead in the 10th inning, but a two-out grounder by Mookie Wilson of the Mets goes through first baseman Bill Buckner's legs. New York wins 6-5.

- The Mets trail Game 7 3-0 after two innings but come back to win the deciding game 8-5, denying Boston its first championship since 1918. Met Ray Knight bats .391 in the Series.

1987

McGwire bursts onto scene... Clemens repeats Cy Young Award... Surprising Twins roll past Cards in Series

- The Cubs' Andre Dawson is named NL MVP.

- George Bell of Toronto is voted AL MVP.

- Boston's Roger Clemens repeats as the AL Cy Young winner.

- Philly's Steve Bedrosian wins the Cy Young in the NL, as he saves an ML-leading 40 games.

- Mark McGwire of the A's is named AL Rookie of the Year, as he hits an ML rookie-record 49 homers and ties Dawson for most homers in the majors.

- San Diego's Tony Gwynn takes the NL bat crown with a .370 BA, highest in the NL since 1948.

- Boston's Wade Boggs wins his fourth AL bat crown in the 1980s (.363).

- Padre catcher Benito Santiago is voted NL Rookie of the Year after setting a frosh record by hitting safely in 34 straight games.

- Cardinal Vince Coleman steals 100 or more bases for an ML-record third straight season.

- Brewer Paul Molitor hits in 39 consecutive games, most in the AL since Joe DiMaggio's 56 in 1941.

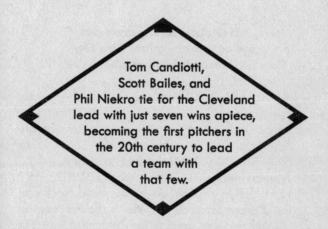

Tom Candiotti, Scott Bailes, and Phil Niekro tie for the Cleveland lead with just seven wins apiece, becoming the first pitchers in the 20th century to lead a team with that few.

- Arbiter Thomas Roberts rules owners guilty of collusion after they fail to sign free agents.

- The NL wins the All-Star Game 2-0 in Oakland, as Tim Raines wins it with a two-run triple in the top of the 13th.

- Yankee Don Mattingly hits six grand slams on the season (setting an ML record) and also hits at least one homer in eight consecutive games (tying an ML record).

- The Brewers tie an ML record by opening the season with 13 consecutive wins.

- Angel Bob Boone sets a career record for backstops when he catches in his 1,919th game.

> **"If (Nolan) Ryan would act his age, there might be a few records left for me."**
>
> —Roger Clemens

- Reggie Jackson retires with an ML career-record 2,597 Ks.

- Toronto hits an ML single-game record 10 homers.

- Cal Ripken Sr. of the Orioles is the first man to manage two sons in the ML—Cal Jr. and Billy. The Ripken sons are the first brothers to form a keystone combo in the majors since Pittsburgh's Johnny and Eddie O'Brien in 1956.

- Cal Ripken's record skein for the most consecutive innings played (8,243) comes to an end.

- Attendance tops 52 million, as the Cardinals and Mets each draw more than three million.

- A record 4,458 homers and 19,883 runs are produced in the majors during the regular season.

- The Twins cop the pennant with a .525 winning pct., lowest ever by a flag winner in the AL. They win just nine road games after the All-Star break, but their 85 total triumphs are enough in the mediocre West.

- Detroit wins the AL East by two games but falls in five in the LCS. Twin Tom Brunansky kills the Tigers with six extra-base hits.

- The Giants whip the Reds by six games in the NL West and take three of the first five LCS games from the Cardinals. St. Louis blanks San Francisco in the final two contests, though, to win its third pennant of the 1980s.

- Home cooking continues to serve the Twins well in the franchise's first Series triumph since the Washington Senators prevailed in 1924. Minnesota wins twice at home, falls three times in St. Louis, and returns to the Metrodome to take the final two. Game 7 is a 4-2 Twins win.

- Frank Viola cops Series MVP accolades with a pair of victories for Minnesota. Kirby Puckett bats .357.

1988

Hershiser strings together 59 goose eggs... Lights go on at Wrigley... Hobbled Gibson homers in a pinch

- LA's Orel Hershiser wins the NL Cy Young. Hershiser sets an ML record with 59 consecutive scoreless innings pitched.

- Minnesota's Frank Viola wins the AL Cy Young. Viola leads the ML with 24 wins and the AL with a .774 winning pct.

- Dodger Kirk Gibson is named NL MVP.

- Oakland's Jose Canseco is named AL MVP, as he becomes the first MLer to steal 40 bases and hit 40 homers in the same season. Canseco tops the majors with 42 homers, 124 RBI, and a .569 SA.

- Walt Weiss is the third consecutive A's player to win AL Rookie of the Year honors.

- The first official night game at Wrigley Field is played on August 9, the Mets vs. Cubs.

- Billy Martin is fired as Yankee manager for a record fifth time.

- The Orioles open the season by losing 21 consecutive games to set an ML record.

- Padre Tony Gwynn leads the NL with a .313 BA, the lowest in history by an NL leader.

- Don Baylor retires with the modern career record for being hit the most times by pitches (267).

- Toronto's George Bell is the first player in ML history to hit three home runs on Opening Day.

- Tom Browning of Cincinnati hurls a perfect game vs. LA on September 16.

- Toronto's Dave Stieb is denied a no-hitter in two consecutive games by two-out, two-strike base hits in the ninth inning.

- David Cone has a 20-3 record for the Mets and tops the NL with an .870 winning pct.

- New York's Darryl Strawberry leads the NL with 39 homers and a .545 SA.

- Wade Boggs paces the AL with a .480 OBP, highest in the majors since Mickey Mantle's .488 in 1962. Boggs also leads the ML in batting (.366), doubles (45), walks (125), and runs (128).

- Expo Andres Galarraga tops the NL in hits (184), doubles (42), and total bases (329).

- Minnesota's Kirby Puckett tops the ML in hits (234), runs produced (206), and total bases (358) and has a .356 BA.

- The Cubs have now gone 43 years without a pennant to break the old ML record of 42 years held by the St. Louis Browns.

- Baseball films *Bull Durham* and *Eight Men Out* are released.

- The Dodgers win the NL West by seven games over the Reds, while the Mets win the East by 15. The two battle for seven games in a coast-to-coast LCS. LA wins the finale thanks to a Hershiser shutout.

- Oakland rides Canseco to an easy AL West title. The only intriguing divisional race is in the AL East, where the Red Sox overtake the Tigers by a single game after Joe Morgan takes over for John McNamara in July. Boston wins 19 of its first 20 games under Morgan.

- The A's sweep the Red Sox in the ALCS.

- A considerable underdog, LA wins the World Series in five games. The tone is set in the opener, when an injured Gibson limps to the plate to pinch hit with two outs in the bottom of the ninth and the Dodgers trailing 4-3. His two-run home run wins the game.

◎ Hershiser wins two complete games in the Series and goes 3-for-3 at the plate.

Kirk Gibson after World Series home run

1989

Quake shakes Bay Area, Series... Rose banned from baseball... Giamatti dies of heart attack

- The Giants' Kevin Mitchell is named NL MVP, as he tops the majors in homers (47), RBI (125), SA (.635), and total bases (345).

- Milwaukee's Robin Yount wins his second AL MVP Award and is the first player to win the honor while playing two different positions.

- KC's Bret Saberhagen wins his second AL Cy Young. Saberhagen leads the majors with 23 wins and has the ML's top winning pct. (.793).

- San Diego reliever Mark Davis wins the Cy Young in the NL. He leads the majors with 44 saves.

- Minnesota's Kirby Puckett tops the ML with a .339 BA and 215 hits.

- Ranger Ruben Sierra leads the AL in SA (.543), RBI (119), triples (14), and total bases (344).

- Texas's Nolan Ryan Ks his 5,000th victim, Rickey Henderson.

- Cardinal Vince Coleman steals an ML-record 50 consecutive bases without being caught.

- Pete Rose is banned from baseball for gambling activities. Commissioner Bart Giamatti dies of a heart attack shortly after banning Rose.

- Boston's Wade Boggs collects 200 hits for a 20th century-record seventh consecutive year. Boggs tops the majors with 51 doubles.

> **"I have concluded that he bet on baseball."**
>
> —*Commissioner Bart Giamatti, addressing the media after his banning of Pete Rose from the game*

- Baltimore's Gregg Olson is named AL Rookie of the Year after he sets a new loop rookie saves record with 27.

- Toronto's Tony Fernandez makes just six errors and sets an ML fielding average record for shortstops (.992).

- Angel Jim Abbott, the first one-handed pitcher since the 1880s, wins 12 games and fans 115.

- Houston's Terry Puhl ends the season with the best career fielding average of any outfielder in ML history (.993).

- Ken Griffey Sr. and Ken Jr. are the first father-and-son tandem in ML history to both be active in the majors at the same time.

- The SkyDome opens on June 5, Milwaukee vs. Toronto. Thanks in part to their new home, the Blue Jays set an AL attendance record.

- Billy Martin dies in a truck crash on Christmas Day.

- San Diego's Tony Gwynn wins the NL bat crown (.336).

- St. Louis's Ozzie Smith sets an ML record for shortstops when he cops his 10th Gold Glove.

- *Field of Dreams*, featuring baseball legend Joe Jackson, is one of the year's top movies.

- The Blue Jays break in their new home by winning the AL East on the final weekend despite a game effort by Baltimore. The A's win the West and take their second straight AL pennant with a five-game LCS win. Toronto's Rickey Henderson steals eight bases and scores eight runs.

- The Cubs win the NL East for the second time in the 1980s, but again make an LCS exit at the hands of a California-based team. This time it's the Giants in five games, as Will Clark sets playoff records for batting average (.650), hits (13), extra-base hits (six), total bases (24), and slugging (1.200).

- On October 17 at 5:04 P.M., an earthquake measuring 7.1 on the Richter Scale rocks the Bay Area about 30 minutes before the scheduled start of Game 3 of the World Series. Commissioner Fay Vincent postpones the Series indefinitely.

- When the Series resumes, Oakland completes a sweep of the most one-sided Series in history. Dave Stewart wins two games for the A's.

World Series quake

Bonds breaks new batting ground... Fielder makes overseas trip pay off... Reds cut off A's power

- Pittsburgh's Barry Bonds is the NL MVP. He becomes the first player in ML history to hit .300 with 30 homers, 100 RBI, and 50 stolen bases.

- Oakland's Rickey Henderson is the AL MVP. He leads the league in runs (119), stolen bases (65), and OBP (.441). Henderson steals his 893rd base, breaking Ty Cobb's AL record.

- Oakland's Bob Welch grabs the AL Cy Young Award after leading the ML in wins (27) and winning pct. (.818). Welch's 27 wins are the most in the majors since 1972.

- Pittsburgh's Doug Drabek wins the NL Cy Young Award. He leads the league in wins (22) and winning pct. (.786).

- On August 17, Carlton Fisk hits his 328th homer as a catcher—an ML record.

- The Royals' George Brett leads the AL in batting (.329), becoming the first player in ML history to win BA titles in three different decades.

- Detroit's Cecil Fielder, after returning from Japan, leads the AL in homers (51), RBI (132), slugging (.592), total bases (339), and strikeouts (182).

- Roger Clemens goes 21-6 for Boston and leads the AL in ERA (1.93).

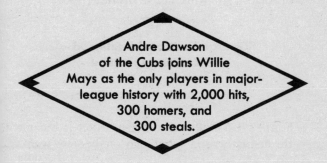

Andre Dawson of the Cubs joins Willie Mays as the only players in major-league history with 2,000 hits, 300 homers, and 300 steals.

- Texas's Nolan Ryan, at age 43, leads his loop in Ks (232) for the 11th time. Ryan also wins his 300th game and fires an ML-record sixth no-hitter vs. the A's on June 11.

- Nine no-hitters are thrown during the season—an ML record. On July 1, Yankee Andy Hawkins no-hits Chicago in a regulation nine-inning game but loses 4-0.

- White Sox Bobby Thigpen breaks the ML save record by 11, as he slams the door 57 times.

- Oakland's Dennis Eckersley saves 48 games, posts a 0.61 ERA, and walks only four batters in 73⅓ innings.

- Chicago's Ryne Sandberg leads the NL in home runs (40), runs (116), and total bases (344).

- Willie McGee, traded from St. Louis to Oakland in August, still wins the NL BA title (.335).

> **"George Brett could get good wood on an aspirin."**
>
> —*Jim Frey*

- Seattle's Ken Griffey Sr. and Ken Griffey Jr. become the first father-son duo to play on the same team.

- Pete Rose is sent to prison for cheating on his taxes.

- On July 17, the Minnesota Twins become the first ML team to make two triple plays in one game.

- After the leagues sign huge new TV contracts, clubs spend their excess millions on free agents. Some salaries soar past the $3-million-a-year mark.

- Commissioner Fay Vincent orders George Steinbrenner to give up controlling interest of the Yankees because of alleged gambling activities.

- Oakland wins 103 games, then takes its third straight AL pennant with its second LCS sweep of Boston in three years.

- The Reds lead the NL West from wire to wire. Their "Nasty Boys" bullpen, featuring Randy Myers and Rob Dibble, rarely blows a lead. The Pirates win the NL East but fall in six games to Cincinnati in the LCS.

- Though Oakland is a big favorite, Cincinnati shocks the baseball world with a Series sweep of the A's. Even more surprising is that the offensive-minded A's muster just eight runs in the Series. Jose Rijo is named MVP with two wins and just one run charged against him.

- Cincinnati's Billy Hatcher hits an all-time World Series-record .750 (9-for-12), as he collects seven hits in his first seven at-bats. Chris Sabo contributes a .563 average and brilliant defense at third base.

1991

Twins, Braves rise from worst to first... Henderson sets thievery mark... Ryan fires seventh no-no

- Cal Ripken of the Orioles wins his second MVP Award, as he extends his consecutive-games-played streak to 1,573. He leads the AL in total bases with 368. Ripken also becomes the first shortstop in AL history to hit .300 with 30 or more homers and 100 or more RBI.

- Third baseman Terry Pendleton of Atlanta wins the NL MVP Award. He cops the hitting crown (.319), tops the loop in hits (187), and ties in total bases (303).

- Boston's Roger Clemens paces the AL in ERA (2.62), strikeouts (241), innings (271), and shutouts (four) and wins his third Cy Young Award.

- Dennis Martinez of the Expos pitches a perfect game against the Dodgers on July 28, winning 2-0. Martinez leads the NL with a 2.39 ERA and five shutouts and also ties in complete games with nine.

- Two days before Martinez's gem, Mark Gardner of the Expos loses a no-hitter to the Dodgers, 1-0 in 10 innings.

- Atlanta's Tom Glavine wins 20 games for the Braves and bags the NL Cy Young Award.

- Howard Johnson of the Mets paces the NL in home runs (38) and RBI (117).

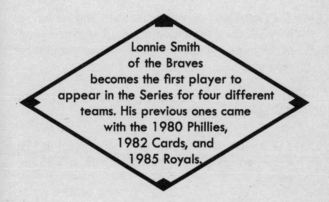

Lonnie Smith of the Braves becomes the first player to appear in the Series for four different teams. His previous ones came with the 1980 Phillies, 1982 Cards, and 1985 Royals.

- The Mets' David Cone ties the NL record when he fans 19 Phillies on the last day of the season.

- Reliever Lee Smith of the Cards sets an NL record when he nets 47 saves.

- Milwaukee's Paul Molitor leads the ML in both runs (133) and hits (216).

- Cecil Fielder of Detroit repeats his 1990 slugging feat when he paces the AL in both homers (44) and RBI (133).

- Texas's Julio Franco wins the AL bat crown (.341).

- Rickey Henderson tops Lou Brock's ML record for career thefts and finishes the season with 994 stolen bases. Henderson also cops his ML-record 11th stolen-base crown (58).

- The Expos have only 68 home dates and are forced to finish their season on the road after a section of Olympic Stadium collapses and cannot be repaired.

- The Blue Jays set an AL attendance record when they draw more than four million fans.

- The Angels (81-81) become the first team in ML history to finish in the basement without a losing record.

- Nolan Ryan throws his ML-record seventh no-hitter on May 1 against the Blue Jays.

- The Braves and Twins rise from last-place divisional finishes in 1990 to capture pennants, becoming the first teams to do so since 1890.

- Atlanta overcomes a 9½-game deficit to catch the Dodgers in the NL West. The Braves need the full seven games to oust the Pirates in the LCS. John Smoltz pitches a 4-0 shutout in the finale to give the team its first flag since moving to Atlanta.

- Minnesota wins 16 games in a row en route to the AL West crown. The Blue Jays claim the AL East but are brushed aside in five games in the LCS.

- In what is considered one of the best World Series ever played, the Twins cop their second title in five years, again without winning on the road.

> Lou Brock needed 19 seasons to set his stolen-base mark of 938, but Rickey Henderson takes just a fraction more than 12 to break it.

- The Series is the first since 1924 to go the ultimate limit—seven games, extra innings, with a win by the home team in the final at-bat. Pinch-hitter Gene Larkin singles home Dan Gladden for a 1-0 Minnesota win in the 10th.

- Jack Morris gets the complete-game win in the finale and is named Series MVP.

1992

Brett, Yount record 3,000th hits... Baseball left without commish... Series trophy moves north of border

- Barry Bonds of the Pirates wins the NL MVP Award. Bonds leads the NL with a .624 SA, 127 walks, .461 OBP, and 109 runs. He signs a $43 million contract with San Francisco after the season.

- Dennis Eckersley of the A's sweeps both the AL Cy Young and MVP Awards. Eck leads the majors with 51 saves.

- The Cubs' Greg Maddux bags the NL Cy Young Award after winning 20 games and posting a 2.18 ERA.

- San Diego's Gary Sheffield rebounds from a miserable .194 season with Milwaukee to lead the league in batting (.330) and total bases (323).

- Fred McGriff of San Diego tops the NL with 35 homers.

- Phillies catcher Darren Daulton leads the NL in RBI with 109.

- Seattle's Edgar Martinez leads the major leagues in batting (.343) and ties in doubles (46).

- Minnesota's Kirby Puckett tops the AL with 210 hits and 313 total bases.

Barry Bonds

- Texas's Juan Gonzalez wins the AL homer title with 43 dingers.

- Cecil Fielder of the Tigers becomes the second player in history to top the ML in RBI three years in a row (124).

- Boston's Roger Clemens tops the AL with five shutouts and a 2.41 ERA.

- Giant Bill Swift tops the ML with a 2.08 ERA.

- Lee Smith of the Cards leads the NL with 43 saves.

- Fay Vincent, under unrelenting pressure from club owners, steps down as commissioner, leaving the game without a titular leader.

- Brewers owner Bud Selig becomes commissioner pro tem.

- Baltimore draws 3,567,819 fans to its new stadium, Oriole Park at Camden Yards.

- George Brett of the Royals and Robin Yount of the Brewers both collect their 3,000th hit.

- Shortstop Ozzie Smith of the Cardinals wins his 13th straight Gold Glove.

- Boston's Jeff Reardon breaks Rollie Fingers's record of 341 career saves.

- Oakland's Rickey Henderson becomes the first player in the ML history to accumulate 1,000 career stolen bases.

- Seattle's Bret Boone joins father Bob and grandfather Ray as the majors' first three-generation family.

- On September 20, second sacker Mickey Morandini of the Phils performs the first unassisted triple play in an NL game since 1927.

- The Pirates win their third consecutive NL East title, but they again fail to win the pennant. This LCS loss hurts more than the others, as seldom-used catcher Francisco Cabrera helps the Braves overcome a 2-1 deficit in the ninth inning of Game 7 with a two-run pinch single off Stan Belinda.

- Toronto repeats in the AL East and hands Oakland a six-game LCS setback.

- Deion Sanders of the Braves plays in a World Series game and an NFL game in the same week.

- Toronto defeats Atlanta in six games, becoming the first team outside the U.S. to win the Series. Dave Winfield clinches it with a two-run, 11th-inning double as the Jays win Game 6 by a 4-3 score.

- Blue Jay catcher Pat Borders bats .450 and is named Series MVP.

1993

Rockies, Marlins join NL ... Ryan hangs up spikes with 5,714 Ks ... Carter blasts Jays to second straight title

- The NL expands to 14 teams, adding the Colorado Rockies and Florida Marlins.

- The Giants' Barry Bonds wins his third NL MVP Award after leading the league in homers (46), RBI (123), slugging (.677), OBP (.458), and total bases (365).

- Chicago's Frank Thomas, with 41 homers and 128 RBI, is the AL MVP.

- Jack McDowell of the White Sox leads the AL in wins (22) and shutouts (four) and takes home the Cy Young Award.

- The Rangers' Juan Gonzalez cops his second straight home run crown (46).

- Seattle's Randy Johnson fans an ML-high 308 batters.

- Cleveland's Albert Belle paces the AL in RBI (129).

- Atlanta's Greg Maddux wins the NL Cy Young Award after topping the circuit in ERA (2.36), innings (267), and complete games (eight).

- Toronto's John Olerud tops the AL in batting (.363), doubles (54), and OBP (.473).

- Andres Galarraga of Colorado smacks .370 to lead the majors.

- Philly's Lenny Dykstra leads the NL in runs (143) and hits (194), then hits four homers in the World Series.

- Toronto's Paul Molitor leads the AL in hits (211) and collects 12 more in 24 at-bats in the World Series.

- The Cubs' Randy Myers tops the majors in saves (53).

- The Rockies yield 927 runs (5.7 per game) but set an ML attendance record (4,483,350).

- Cleveland pitchers Steve Olin and Tim Crews are killed in a boating accident in spring training. Bob Ojeda survives the crash and returns to the mound in August.

- The Tigers' 899 runs scored are the most in the majors since 1953.

- The Mets' Vince Coleman is sentenced to three years probation after throwing a firecracker at a group of fans.

- In February, Reds owner Marge Schott is suspended for one year for using ethnic slurs.

- Dodgers catcher Mike Piazza is the unanimous choice for the NL Rookie of the Year Award after hitting .318 with 35 homers.

- The major leagues go the entire season without a commissioner.

- Met pitcher Anthony Young loses his 27th consecutive game—an ML record.

- Montreal's Curtis Pride, born without hearing, doubles in his ML debut.

- Nolan Ryan retires as the ML leader in strikeouts with 5,714 (1,578 more than anyone else) and walks with 2,795.

- On September 7, St. Louis's Mark Whiten hits four homers with 12 RBI against the Reds.

- Philadelphia wins the NL East while the Braves again take the West. Atlanta does it with 104 wins, one better than second-place San Francisco. The Phillies capture the LCS in six games, beating Maddux in the finale.

- The White Sox and Blue Jays win their AL divisions. The Jays garner their second straight pennant with a six-game LCS victory. Pitcher Dave Stewart improves to 8-0 in ALCS games.

- The Blue Jays make it back-to-back Series titles with a six-game triumph. Joe Carter gives the set a dramatic ending when he belts a three-run homer off Mitch Williams in the bottom of the ninth for an 8-6 win.

Joe Carter after World Series home run

1994

*Strike wipes out World Series... "Big Hurt"
wins second straight MVP... Jordan shoots
Double-A airball*

- Each league breaks into three divisions. Six division winners plus two wild-card teams are scheduled to make the playoffs.

- The average ML salary is an estimated $1.2 million.

- Unable to reach a basic agreement, the major-league players strike on August 12. The owners want to impose a salary cap, but the players won't give in. On September 14, the season is officially canceled.

- Chicago's Frank Thomas wins his second straight MVP Award. He leads the AL in slugging (.729), walks (109), and OBP (.487) and belts 38 homers.

- The NL MVP is Houston's Jeff Bagwell, who hits 39 homers and leads the loop in RBI (116), runs (104), and SA (.750—the highest mark since Babe Ruth).

- Atlanta's Greg Maddux wins his third straight Cy Young after leading the NL in ERA (1.56) and complete games (10) and tying in wins (16).

- Kansas City's David Cone cops the AL Cy Young Award.

- Jacobs Field in Cleveland and The Ballpark at Arlington open for play.

- Basketball star Michael Jordan, age 31, signs with the Chicago White Sox and is assigned to Double-A Birmingham, where he bats .202 over a full season.

> **"The last time the Cubs won the World Series was 1908. The last time they were in one was 1945. Hey, any team can have a bad century."**
>
> —New Cubs manager Tom Trebelhorn

- Cubs superstar Ryne Sandberg, age 34, abruptly retires in June.

- On July 9, Boston shortstop John Valentin performs an unassisted triple play.

- On July 28, Texas's Kenny Rogers tosses a perfect game against California.

- Matt Williams of the Giants leads the ML in homers (43).

- San Diego's Tony Gwynn wins his fifth BA title (.394) and also leads in OBP (.454).

- Yankee Paul O'Neill tops the AL in hitting (.359).

- Seattle's Ken Griffey Jr. paces the AL in homers (40).

- The Twins' Kirby Puckett leads the AL in RBI (112).

- Cleveland's Kenny Lofton leads the AL in hits (160) and stolen bases (60).

- The Indians' Albert Belle hits .357 with 36 homers and 101 RBI. He is suspended for a week in July, however, for using a corked bat in a game against the White Sox.

- The Mets' Bret Saberhagen wins 14 games and walks just 13 batters.

- Cubs broadcaster Harry Caray celebrates his 50th year in the booth.

- Mets pitcher Dwight Gooden checks into the Betty Ford Center for treatment of substance abuse, then violates his aftercare program. In November, he gets a season-long suspension.

- Moises Alou doubles home Gwynn in the 10th inning of the All-Star Game for an 8-7 NL win that snaps the AL's six-game winning streak.

- Tiles fall from the Kingdome roof, halting a July game between the Mariners and Orioles. The Mariners become a permanent road team. In August, two construction workers are killed when the basket on their crane falls 250 feet.

- Ken Burns's *Baseball*, a nine-part documentary that airs on PBS in September, helps fill the baseball void created by the strike.

- At Boston's Fenway Park, Leslie Sterling becomes the AL's first female public-address announcer.

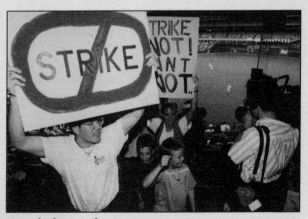

Fans before strike

Maddux makes it four in a row... Ripken breaks Gehrig's record... Braves' pitching too much for Indians

- In January, the 64 AL and NL umpires are locked out by baseball owners. It ends May 1, one week into the season.

- Replacement players are used in spring training because of the continuing player strike. A 234-day work stoppage ends on April 2, the day the season was supposed to begin, and Opening Day is set for April 25.

- Boston first baseman Mo Vaughn wins the AL MVP Award after tying for the AL lead in RBI (126) and leading Boston to the AL East flag.

- Barry Larkin of the Reds is selected as the NL MVP. He finishes fifth in batting (.319) and fifth in runs (98) and leads Cincinnati to an NL Central title.

- Dante Bichette of the Rockies is tops in the NL with a .620 SA, 40 homers, and 128 RBI.

- The Indians' Albert Belle becomes the first player in history to collect 50 home runs and 50 doubles in the same season. He also is the first player since Stan Musial in 1948 to bag 100 or more extra-base hits. Belle leads the AL with a .690 SA and 126 RBI (tied with Mo Vaughn).

- Greg Maddux of the Braves is the first pitcher ever to win four straight Cy Young Awards. Because two of his crowns come in strike-shortened seasons, Maddux has the added distinction of being a four-time Cy Young recipient despite only twice being a 20-game winner.

- Los Angeles backstopper Mike Piazza notches a .346 batting average. It is the highest in history by an NL catcher with 400 or more at-bats.

- Randy Johnson of Seattle leads the AL in strikeouts (294) for the fourth consecutive year. His 12.35 strikeouts per nine innings breaks Nolan Ryan's 1987 record of 11.48. Johnson also tops the loop with a 2.48 ERA.

- Seattle DH Edgar Martinez leads the AL with a .356 batting average and a .479 on-base average, and he ties Belle for the loop lead with 126 runs scored and 52 doubles.

- Indians reliever Jose Mesa breaks Dennis Eckersley's 1992 record (36) when he converts 38 straight save opportunities.

Cal Ripken after breaking Lou Gehrig's consecutive-games record

- Cal Ripken of the Orioles breaks Lou Gehrig's record when he appears in his 2,131st straight game on September 6 against the Angels.

- Lou Whitaker and Alan Trammell of the Tigers set an AL record for the most games by a pair of teammates when they're both in the Detroit lineup for the 1,915th time on September 13 against Milwaukee.

- Tony Gwynn of the Padres becomes only the seventh player in ML history to capture six or more batting titles. He is also the first National Leaguer since Rogers Hornsby in 1929 to hit .350 or better three years in a row.

- Los Angeles rookie hurler Hideo Nomo uses his whirling windup to confuse NL batters. He finishes second to Maddux in loop ERA (2.54) while leading the league in strikeouts (236).

- Eddie Murray of the Indians collects his 3,000th hit.

- Mickey Mantle dies of liver cancer at age 63.

- The Yankees and Mariners play a dramatic Division Series in the first year of the expanded playoffs. Seattle comes back from a 2-0 deficit in the best-of-five, winning the finale 6-5 in 11 innings.

- The Braves sweep the Reds in the NLCS. The Indians stop the Mariners in six ALCS games.

- For the first time since moving to Atlanta, the Braves are World Series champs. They win in six games over Cleveland. The last one is a 1-0 shutout by Tom Glavine and Mark Wohlers.

1996

Homers soar like never before ... Gwynn wins seventh hitting title ... Wetteland saves day for champion Yanks

- Colorado's Ellis Burks leads the NL with a .639 slugging percentage, 142 runs, and 392 total bases—most in the NL since Henry Aaron had 400 for the 1959 Milwaukee Braves.

- Ken Caminiti wins the NL MVP Award. He bats .326 with 40 homers and 130 RBI in leading the upstart Padres to the NL West title.

- Juan Gonzalez caps the AL MVP Award after amassing 47 homers and 144 RBI in 134 games.

- Oakland's Mark McGwire leads the majors in home runs (52) and slugging (.730).

- Toronto's Pat Hentgen, 20-10, bags the AL Cy Young Award.

- Andy Pettitte of the Yankees finishes 21-8 in his second ML season.

- Alex Rodriguez of Seattle paces the AL with a .358 average, 141 runs, 54 doubles, and 379 total bases.

- John Smoltz of the Braves wins the Cy Young Award. He goes 24-8 and leads the majors in victories and strikeouts (276).

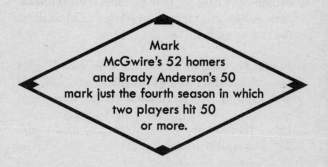

Mark McGwire's 52 homers and Brady Anderson's 50 mark just the fourth season in which two players hit 50 or more.

- Brady Anderson of the Orioles hits an ML-record 12 of his 50 home runs leading off games.

- Tony Gwynn of San Diego hits .353 to win his seventh NL batting title.

- San Francisco's Barry Bonds becomes the fourth ML player to notch 300 career homers and 300 stolen bases, following his godfather Willie Mays, his father Bobby Bonds, and Andre Dawson. Barry also joins Jose Canseco's exclusive 40-40 club with 42 homers and 40 steals.

- John Wetteland notches an AL-best 43 saves during the regular season, then saves all four Yankee wins in being named World Series MVP.

- Eddie Murray of Baltimore joins Hank Aaron and Willie Mays as the only ML players with 500 home runs and 3,000 hits.

- Minnesota's Paul Molitor becomes the 21st MLer with 3,000 hits, rapping an AL-best 225 to finish the season with 3,014.

- Frank Thomas of the White Sox has 20-plus homers and doubles and 100-plus runs, RBI, and walks for an ML-record sixth straight year.

- Lance Johnson of the Mets leads the majors with 227 hits and 21 triples.

- Roger Clemens of the Red Sox records 20 strikeouts at Detroit on September 18 to tie his own 1986 record for Ks in a nine-inning game.

- Umpire John McSherry dies of a heart attack while working an Opening Day game at Cincinnati.

- The Orioles, Mariners, and A's all break the ML home run record of 240.

- The Rockies become the second team in ML history with three 40-homer men—Ellis Burks, Andres Galarraga, and Vinny Castilla.

- Mel Allen, longtime voice of the Yankees, dies at age 83.

- Andres Galarraga leads the NL with 47 homers and 150 RBI—the most in the ML since Tommy Davis's 153 for the '62 Dodgers.

- The Mets and Padres play a June game in Monterey, Mexico, the first regular-season game played outside the U.S. or Canada.

- On September 27, Baltimore's Roberto Alomar spits in the face of umpire John Hirschbeck after being ejected for arguing a called third strike.

- The Yankees defeat the Rangers in the Division Series, then take five games to oust the Orioles in the ALCS. The Braves beat the Dodgers in the Division Series before a seven-game NLCS win over St. Louis.

- The Series title goes to the Yankees for the first time in 18 years. In a six-game win over the Braves, New York gets .391 hitting from Cecil Fielder.

- Yankee manager Joe Torre celebrates the emotional Series win while his brother, Frank, recuperates from heart-transplant surgery.

1997

Marlins land the big one in just five years... AL meets NL in regular season... Clemens grabs fourth Cy Young

- Interleague play debuts with a 4-3 win by host Texas over San Francisco on June 12.

- The Mariners' Ken Griffey Jr. is the unanimous AL MVP after leading the league with 56 homers (most in the AL since 1961) and 147 RBI.

- The NL MVP goes to Colorado's Larry Walker, who hits .366 with 130 RBI and a league-high 49 homers. He also leads in slugging (.720) and on-base pct. (.452). His 409 total bases are the most in the majors since 1948.

- Toronto's Roger Clemens wins his record-tying fourth Cy Young Award and becomes the first pitcher since 1945 to lead the AL in wins (21), ERA (2.05), and strikeouts (292).

- Rookie Scott Rolen has 21 homers, 92 RBI, and 35 doubles for last-place Philadelphia.

- Pedro Martinez of the Expos captures the NL Cy Young Award with 305 strikeouts and an ML-best 1.90 ERA.

- Mark McGwire belts 58 homers for Oakland and St. Louis—the most in the ML since Roger Maris's 61 in 1961.

- Boston's Nomar Garciaparra has an AL rookie-record 30-game hit streak. He tops the league with 209 hits and 11 triples and sets a record for lead-off men with 98 RBI.

- Frank Thomas of the White Sox wins his first AL batting crown with a .347 average.

- San Diego's Tony Gwynn leads the NL with a .372 average and becomes the third player to win at least eight batting titles.

- Houston's Craig Biggio tops the majors with 146 runs.

- Phillies pitcher Curt Schilling fans 319 batters, the most ever by an NL right-hander.

- The Mariners set an ML record with 264 home runs.

- The Orioles become the third team in AL history to hold first place each day of the season, joining the '27 Yankees and '84 Tigers.

- Dodgers catcher Mike Piazza raps .362 with 201 hits, 40 homers, and 124 RBI in what is considered the greatest offensive season ever for a backstop.

- Baseball celebrates the 50th anniversary of Jackie Robinson's major-league debut.

> **"This is for all the minor-league managers, the guys in the instructional leagues. I'm a Double-A backup, funky catcher. So don't give up, guys."**
>
> —*Florida manager Jim Leyland*

- Atlanta and Florida sweep Houston and San Francisco, respectively, in NL Division Series. Despite 101 wins during the regular season, the Braves fall to the wild-card Marlins in six LCS games.

- With just an 86-75 record, Cleveland wins its third straight AL Central title. The Indians need five games for a Division Series win over the Yankees, then beat Baltimore in six in the LCS.

- Orioles pitcher Mike Mussina sets an ALCS record with 15 strikeouts in Game 3.

- The Florida Marlins, with the help of an $89 million spending spree during the off-season, win a World Series title in their fifth year of existence.

- A fairly dull Series for six games becomes a thriller in Game 7. It's the fourth World Series in history to feature an extra-inning Game 7, which the Marlins win 3-2. Florida scores with one out in the ninth to tie the game. An 11th-inning error by Cleveland's Tony Fernandez sets up Edgar Renteria's game-winning hit off Charles Nagy.

- Florida pitcher Livan Hernandez is named MVP of the NLCS and World Series, winning two games in each set.

Ken Griffey Jr.

1998

Big Mac outslugs Sosa, Maris... Ripken takes a well-earned rest... Yankees win 125 total games

- Mark McGwire of St. Louis blasts 70 home runs, shattering Roger Maris's ML record of 61 set in 1961. McGwire beats out Cub Sammy Sosa, who also breaks the old record with 66 homers.

- Sammy Sosa is named NL MVP, leading Chicago to the playoffs with 158 RBI—most in the ML in 50 seasons. Sosa's 20 home runs in June set a one-month homer record.

- The world champion Yankees set an ML record with 125 total victories and an AL mark with 114 regular-season wins.

- Expansion teams in Arizona (NL West) and Tampa Bay (AL East) boost ML membership to 30. Both clubs finish last.

- Tom Glavine of Atlanta wins his second Cy Young Award by going 20-6 with a 2.47 ERA.

- Oriole Cal Ripken voluntarily ends his record streak of 2,632 consecutive games played on September 20 in Baltimore.

- The Milwaukee Brewers become the first team since the inception of the AL in 1901 to switch leagues, moving from the AL Central to the NL Central.

- Juan Gonzalez of the Rangers tallies a record 35 RBI in April, drives in 157 runs overall, and wins his second MVP Award in three years.

- Blue Jay Roger Clemens earns his record fifth Cy Young, leading the AL in wins (20), ERA (2.65), and strikeouts (271) for the second straight year. Clemens goes 15-0 after May 29.

- Cubs 20-year-old rookie Kerry Wood ties Clemens's ML record with 20 strikeouts in a nine-inning game vs. Houston on May 6. He finishes with 233 strikeouts in just 166⅔ innings.

- David Wells of the Yankees pitches the 13th perfect game in ML history, vs. the Twins on May 17.

- Seattle's Alex Rodriguez amasses 42 homers and 46 steals, becoming the third member of the 40-40 club.

- Bud Selig is officially named baseball's ninth commissioner after six interim years at the post.

Mark McGwire

- Craig Biggio of Houston is the second player in the 20th century with 50 steals and 50 doubles in one year.

- Two famous Chicago Cubs broadcasters die— Harry Caray in February and Jack Brickhouse in August.

- Trevor Hoffman leads the ML with 53 saves for San Diego.

- Tom Gordon of the Red Sox sets an ML mark by converting 43 straight saves. Fellow Boston reliever Dennis Eckersley's last regular-season appearance is his 1,071st, also an ML record.

- Indians outfielder Mark Whitten takes the mound on a lark and strikes out the side against Oakland on July 31.

- The Cubs and Giants each lose on the final day of the regular season, forcing a one-game playoff for the NL wild card. Chicago prevails 5-3 for its first playoff trip since 1989.

- Atlanta wins a franchise-record 106 games, but it falls short of its World Series goal for the second straight season. With Sterling Hitchcock winning two NLCS starts, the Padres oust the Braves in six games for their second trip to the Series in their 30-year existence.

- The Yankees win 11 of 13 postseason games, including four straight over San Diego in the World Series. It's the 24th world championship in franchise history.

- Yankee Scott Brosius is named World Series MVP. The unheralded third baseman hits .471 with two home runs and six RBI.

1999

McGwire, Sosa play an encore... Umpires make ultimate bad call... Yanks win 25th world title

- Mark McGwire of the Cardinals again edges the Cubs' Sammy Sosa to win the ML home run title. McGwire finishes with 65 to Sosa's 63, as they become the only men in history to record back-to-back seasons of 60 or more.

- McGwire's 70th home run ball from the 1998 season goes at an auction for $2.7 million, 23 times the record for any previous baseball item.

- Manny Ramirez of the Indians drives in 165 runs, most in the majors since Jimmie Foxx's 175 in 1938.

- Colorado's Larry Walker leads the NL with a .379 average. Nomar Garciaparra of the Red Sox paces the AL at .357.

- A day apart, the Padres' Tony Gwynn and Devil Rays' Wade Boggs record their 3,000th career hits.

- Two pitchers notch 300 strikeouts. Randy Johnson of the Diamondbacks fans 364 to lead the NL. Pedro Martinez of the Red Sox tops the AL with 313, and his minuscule 2.07 ERA is less than half of the ML average.

- Baseball's opening pitch comes outside the U.S. or Canada for the first time ever, as Colorado defeats San Diego in Mexico on April 4.

- In what is meant as a bargaining ploy, ML umpires make a June announcement that they plan to resign in September. The move fails mightily. Baseball accepts several resignations, promotes umps from the minors, and receives the fans' overwhelming support.

- The Baltimore Orioles take baseball to Cuba, defeating that country's national team by a 3-2 score in a March exhibition. In May, the Cubans defeat the Orioles 12-6 in Baltimore.

- Hideki Irabu and Mac Suzuki oppose one another in the first-ever ML matchup of Japanese starters.

- The Mets' Robin Ventura becomes the first player in either league to slug grand slams in both games of a doubleheader.

- David Cone fires the 14th perfect game in history, a 6-0 win over Montreal on July 18 (Yogi Berra Day) at Yankee Stadium.

- Cardinal Fernando Tatis, who had never before hit a grand slam, becomes the first player in history to hit two in the same inning. Both come off Dodger pitcher Chan Ho Park. His eight RBI in the inning also set a major-league record.

- Joe DiMaggio dies at age 84.

- Roger Clemens, acquired by the Yankees from Toronto in a big trade before the season, sets an AL record by winning 20 consecutive decisions.

Sammy Sosa

- Two 1999 playoff managers miss time while hospitalized. Houston's Larry Dierker seizes during a game and undergoes brain surgery before returning. Joe Torre of the Yankees learns he has prostate cancer and starts the year away from the ballpark.

- Torre's Yankees sweep the Rangers in the Division Series, while Boston rides a 23-7 win in Game 4 to oust Cleveland in the other AL series.

- New York requires just five games to oust the wild-card Red Sox in the ALCS.

- The Mets, losers of seven straight games down the stretch, recover on the final weekend to force a one-game playoff with the Reds for the NL wild-card berth. They defeat Cincy, then down Arizona in the Division Series.

- Atlanta knocks off Houston in the Division Series before surviving the Mets in a hotly contested six-game NLCS.

- The Yankees win their third world title in four years and 25th of the 1900s, sweeping the Braves in four. In doing so, they stretch their Series win streak to 12 games. Stopper Mariano Rivera, with a win and two saves, earns Series MVP honors.

Index

A
Aaron, Hank, 195, 198, 204, 206, 222, 237, 240, 244, 253, 264, 266, 267, 275
Abbott, Jim, 327
Abernathy, Ted, 231
Acosta, Mel, 48
Adams, Ace, 144
Adams, Babe, 36
Adcock, Joe, 186
Aikens, Willie, 304
Aker, Jack, 236
Alexander, Dale, 96
Alexander, Pete, 40, 41, 50, 52, 55, 57, 58, 65, 68, 87
Allen, Dick, 227, 258, 267
Allen, Johnny, 119
Allen, Lee, 86
Allen, Mel, 357
All-Star Game, 106, 144, 151, 179, 208
Alomar, Roberto, 357
Alou, Felipe, 224, 236
Alou, Matty, 224, 236
Alou, Moises, 224, 349
Alston, Walter, 191, 233, 276
Altobelli, Joe, 305
Altrock, Nick, 107
American Baseball Guild, 156
Ames, Leon, 35
Anaheim Stadium (Los Angeles), 236
Anderson, Brady, 355
Anderson, Sparky, 257, 309
Andrews, Mike, 265
Andujar, Joaquin, 301
Antonelli, Johnny, 187, 189
Aparicio, Luis, 196, 209, 225, 227
Appling, Luke, 115, 142
Arizona Diamondbacks, 362, 369
Arlin, Harold, 71
Armas, Tony, 307
Arroyo, Luis, 216
Ashburn, Richie, 190, 203
Ashford, Emmett, 232
Astrodome (Houston), 232, 275
Atlanta Braves, 236, 249, 264, 276, 284, 298, 300, 336, 341, 344, 353, 357, 360, 365, 369
Avila, Bobby, 187

B
Bad News Bears (movie), 276
Bagby, Jim, 68
Bagwell, Jeff, 346
Bailes, Scott, 319
Baker, Del, 132
Baker, Dusty, 279, 281
Baker, Frank "Home Run," 39, 42, 45, 47, 48, 53
Baker Bowl (Philadelphia), 17, 123
Ball, Neal, 35
Ballpark at Arlington, The, 347
Baltimore (AL), 16
Baltimore Orioles, 186, 188, 237, 249, 250, 253, 257, 268, 269, 289, 305, 323, 340, 356, 359, 367
Bankhead, Dan, 161
Banks, Ernie, 192, 195, 202, 206, 207, 211
Barber, Steve, 239
Barfield, Jesse, 316
Barker, Len, 296
Barr, Jim, 260
Barrett, Red, 148
Bartell, Dick, 121
Baseball (documentary), 349
Baseball National Commission, 49
Bates, Johnny, 25
Bauer, Hank, 173
Bauman, Joe, 189

Bay, Harry, 17
Baylor, Don, 286, 323
Bearden, Gene, 162
Beaumont, Ginger, 14, 16
Beazley, Johnny, 139, 141, 145
Beckley, Jake, 26
Bedrosian, Steve, 318
Bedzek, Hugo, 58
Belinda, Stan, 341
Belinsky, Bo, 220
Bell, Beau, 120
Bell, George, 318, 323
Belle, Albert, 343, 348, 351
Bench, Johnny, 250, *251*, 258, 268, 277
Bentley, Jack, 77
Benton, Al, 180
Benton, Larry, 92
Berger, Wally, 99, 114
Berra, Yogi, 173, 174, 181, 186, 190, 197, 231
Bevens, Bill, 161
Bichette, Dante, 350
Biggio, Craig, 359, 364
Big Red Machine, 272, 277
Black, Joe, 181
"Black Sox" scandal, 66, 67
Blackwell, Ewell, 160
Blair, Paul, 237
Blass, Steve, 257
Blomberg, Ron, 263
Blue, Vida, 254, 257, 260, 274, 284, 295
Blyleven, Bert, 316
Boggs, Wade, 303, 310, 315, 318, 323, 327, 366
Bonds, Barry, 330, 338, *339*, 342, 355
Bonds, Bobby, 249, 252, 264, 282
Bonham, Tiny, 141
Boone, Bob, 320, 341
Boone, Bret, 341
Boone, Ike, 95
Boone, Ray, 341
Bordagaray, Frenchy, 122
Borders, Pat, 341
Borowy, Hank, 141

Bostock, Lyman, 283
Boston Braves, 23, 45, 49, 51, 93, 112, 114, 119, 164, 183
Boston Massacre, 285
Boston Pilgrims, 17, 18, 21
Boston Red Sox, 29, 33, 45, 54, 57, 62, 63, 86, 104, 108, 157, 168, 169, 178, 184, 239, 241, 272, 279, 280, 285, 317, 324, 369
Boswell, Dave, 248
Bottomley, Jim, 80, 86, 91
Boudreau, Lou, 132, 139, 146, 162, 164-165
Bowa, Larry, 255, 287, 312
Boyer, Ken, 226
Bradley, Alva, 130
Branca, Ralph, 176
Braun, Steve, 275
Braves Field (Boston), 117
Brazle, Alpha, 145
Brecheen, Harry, 145, 157, 164
Brett, George, 274-275, 290, *292*, 303, 313, 331, 332, 340
Brickhouse, Jack, 364
Bridges, Tommy, 114, 117
Bridwell, Al, 32
Brinkman, Ed, 260
Britton, Helen, 42
Brock, Lou, 241, 245, 256, 266, 288, 337
Broglio, Ernie, 212
Brooklyn Dodgers, 32, 57, 124, 126, 136, 137, 138, 157, 161, 169, 179, 181, 183, 185, 187, 191, 193, 196, 197, 199
Brooklyn Robins, 69
Brosius, Scott, 365
Brown, Mace, 124
Brown, Three Finger, 25, 33, 35
Brown, Tommy, 150
Browning, Tom, 323
Brunansky, Tom, 321
Bruton, Billy, 192
Bryant, Clay, 124
Bryant, Ron, 262
Buckner, Bill, 292, 316, 317

Buhl, Bob, 220
Bull Durham (movie), 324
Bunker, Wally, 226
Bunning, Jim, 227
Burdette, Lew, 201
Burkett, Jesse, 10
Burks, Ellis, 354, 356
Burnett, Johnny, 105
Burns, George, 77, 83, 85
Burroughs, Jeff, 266
Busch Stadium (St. Louis), 236

C

Cabrera, Francisco, 341
Cadore, Leon, 68
Cady, Hack, 54
Calbert, Ernie, 60
California Angels, 210, 214, 219, 257, 289, 301, 336
Camilli, Dolph, 134
Caminiti, Ken, 354
Campanella, Roy, 174, 182, *183*, 190, 203, 208
Campaneris, Bert, 231
Candelaria, John, 280
Candiotti, Tom, 319
Canseco, Jose, 314, 322, 324, 355
Capra, Buzz, 269
Caray, Harry, 348, 364
Carew, Rod, 238, 247, 260, 264, 266, 278, 279, 282, 289, 312
Carey, Max, 75, 83
Carlton, Steve, 249, 258, 259, 261, 278, 290, 293, 295, 298, 302, 307, 316
Carter, Gary, 308
Carter, Joe, 345, *345*
Carty, Rico, 251
Case, George, 143
Casey, Hugh, 137
Cash, Dave, 271
Cash, Norm, 215
Castilla, Vinny, 356
Cavarretta, Phil, 150, 153
Cepeda, Orlando, 202, 216, 238
Cey, Ron, 279

Chalmers Award, 40, 53
Chambliss, Chris, 277
Chance, Dean, 227
Chance, Frank, 15, 26, 33, 39, 48, 49
Chandler, Happy, 151, 160, 171, 174
Chandler, Spud, 141, 142, 145, *145*, 160
Chapman, Ray, 67
Chase, Hal, 55
Chech, Charlie, 34
Cheney, Tom, 219
Chesbro, Jack, 12, 13, 19
Chicago Cubs, 13, 23, 25, 27, 30, 32, 33, 35, 39, 42, 62, 63, 70, 73, 96, 105, 114, 125, 132, 152, 153, 232, 296, 309, 324, 329, 347, 365
Chicago Whales, 50, 53
Chicago White Sox, 12, 23, 25, 27, 53, 60, 62, 65, 66, 67, 68, 74, 103, 143, 176, 201, 208, 209, 296, 305, 345
Cicotte, Eddie, 58, *59*, 65, 67
Cincinnati Reds, 56, 65, 66, 68, 108, 111, 114, 126, 129, 131, 132, 194, 195, 196, 199, 204, 217, 229, 253, 261, 265, 272, 273, 276, 277, 280, 294, 333, 369
Clark, Will, 329
Clarke, Nig, 14, 24
Clemens, Roger, 314, 318, 320, 331, 334, 340, 356, 358, 363, 368
Clemente, Roberto, 215, 235, 240, 247, 256, 257, 259
Cleveland (AL), 20
Cleveland Indians, 53, 55, 63, 68, 69, 77, 96, 126, 130, 132, 152, 164-165, 175, 189, 196, 224, 240, 268, 271, 279, 353, 360, 369
Cleveland Naps, 23, 30
Cloninger, Tony, 235
Coakley, Andy, 24
Coastal Plains League, 156

Cobb, Ty, 28, 31, 34, 38, 42, 43, 45, 46, 51, 52, 58, 61, 64, 72, 77, 84, 89, 90, 92, 116, 216
Cochrane, Mickey, 91, 109, 119, 289
Colavito, Rocky, 208, 211
Colbert, Nate, 260
Cole, King, 38
Coleman, Jerry, 173
Coleman, Vince, 311, 319, 327, 344
Coliseum (Los Angeles), 208, 209
Collins, Eddie, 39, 45, 50, 83, 92
Collins, Jimmy, 27
Collins, Ripper, 111
Colorado Rockies, 342, 343, 356, 367
Comiskey, Charlie, 74
Comiskey Park (Chicago), 37, 39, 304
Cone, David, 323, 335, 347, 367
Conigliaro, Billy, 252
Conigliaro, Tony, 227, 232, 239, 252
Connor, Roger, 70
Coombs, Jack, 26, 37
Cooney, Jimmy, 90
Cooper, Cecil, 292, 301
Cooper, Mort, 138
Cooper, Walker, 142, 145, 152, 168
Corriden, John, 38
Coveleski, Stan, 69
Cox, William, 144
Craig, Roger, 223
Cramer, Doc, 125
Cravath, Gavvy, 47, 52, 59, 60
Crawford, Sam, 32, 38, 56
Crews, Tim, 343
Cronin, Joe, 108, 110, 143, 157, 206
Crosby, Bing, 156
Crosley, Powell, 108
Crosley Field (Cincinnati), 43, 114
Crowder, Al, 103, 106

Cuban national team, 367
Cuellar, Mike, 247

D
Dark, Alvin, 162, 269
Daubert, Jake, 46
Daulton, Darren, 339
Davalillo, Vic, 252
Davenport, Jim, 244
Davis, Harry, 21, 22, 29
Davis, Mark, 326
Davis, Tommy, 218, 223
Davis, Willie, 248
Dawson, Andre, 318, 331
Dean, Dizzy, 104, 107, 109, 110, 111, 112, 124
Dean, Paul, 110, 111
Delahanty, Ed, 13, 16
Dempsey, Rick, 305
Denehy, Bill, 239
Denkinger, Don, 313
Denny, John, 302
Dent, Bucky, 285
Derringer, Paul, 126, 133
Derrington, Jim, 195
Detroit Tigers, 30, 33, 36, 54, 71, 78, 111, 114, 132, 136, 152, 245, 271, 306, 309, 324, 343
Devery, Bill, 17
Dibble, Rob, 333
Dickey, Bill, 121, 144
Dierker, Larry, 369
DiMaggio, Dom, 157, 164, 168
DiMaggio, Joe, 110, 116, 120, 121, 126, 131, 134, *135*, 136, 141, 158, 164, 167, 171, 173, 177, 189, 368
Dinneen, Bill, 21
Doby, Larry, 160, 181, 187
Dodger Stadium (Los Angeles), 220
Doscher, Jack, 18
Doubleday, Abner, 30
Douthit, Taylor, 93
Downing, Al, 266
Doyle, Larry, 43, 52
Drabek, Doug, 330

Driessen, Dan, 277
Dropo, Walt, 180
Drysdale, Don, 218, 234, 242
Duren, Ryne, 204
Durocher, Leo, 137, 160, 161
Dykes, Jimmy, 103, 211
Dykstra, Lenny, 343

E

Earnshaw, George, 94, 99, 102
Ebbets, Charlie, 35, 47
Ebbets Field (Brooklyn), 46, 126, 169, 173, 181
Eckersley, Dennis, 332, 338, 365
Eckert, Spike, 231, 246
Eight Men Out (movie), 324
Elberfeld, Kid, 32
Elliott, Bob, 158
Erskine, Carl, 184
Etten, Nick, 147
Evans, Darrell, 264, 312
Evans, Dwight, 307
Evers, Johnny, 15, 33, 49, 50

F

Faber, Red, 60, 71, 75
Face, Elroy, 208, 220
Fain, Ferris, 176, 178
Fairly, Ron, 233
Faul, Bill, 232
Federal League, 48, 49, 50, 53
Feller, Bob, 116, 121, 124, 128, 131, *133*, 136, 154, 155, 165, 175
Felton, Terry, 300
Fenway Park (Boston), 43, 154, 164, 172, 285, 349
Fernandez, Tony, 327, 361
Ferrell, Frank, 17
Ferrell, Rick, 108
Ferrell, Wes, 102, 108, 112, 136
Ferriss, Boo, 152
Fette, Lou, 119
Fidrych, Mark, 275, 280
Fielder, Cecil, 331, 336, 340, 357
Field of Dreams (movie), 328
Fingers, Rollie, 274, 285, 294, 299

Finley, Charles, 265, 274, 296
Fisk, Carlton, 260, 272, 273, 330
Flanagan, Mike, 286
Flick, Elmer, 22
Flood, Curt, 245, 248
Florida Marlins, 342, 360, 361
Forbes Field (Pittsburgh), 34, 112, 113, 213
Ford, Whitey, 173, 191, 193, 196, 204, 215, 217, 221, 225, 239
Foster, George, 278, 283
Foster, Rube, 54, 68
Fox, Nellie, 200, 203, 206
Foxx, Jimmie, 99, 103, 106, 110, 114, 122, *123*, 127, 241, 366
Foytack, Paul, 224
Franco, Julio, 336
Fraser, Chick, 12
Fraternity of Professional Baseball Players of America, 49
Frazier, George, 297
Frederick, Johnny, 83, 95, 105
Freeman, Buck, 16
Fregosi, Jim, 257
Frey, Jim, 309, 332
Frick, Ford, 174, 199, 231
Friend, Bob, 193, 203
Frisch, Frankie, 78, 87, 100, 102
Fuchs, Emil "Judge," 95
Fulton County Stadium (Atlanta), 236
Furillo, Carl, 182

G

Gaedel, Eddie, 175
Gaetti, Gary, 295
Galarraga, Andres, 324, 343, 356, 357
Galbreath, John, 156
Gammons, Peter, 316
Garcia, Mike, 175, 179, 187
Garciaparra, Nomar, 359, 366
Gardella, Danny, 171
Gardner, Larry, 53
Gardner, Mark, 335

Garms, Debs, 131
Garr, Ralph, 268
Garvey, Steve, 266, 279, 285, 297, 302, 312
Gashouse Gang,
Gedeon, Elmer, 147
Gehrig, Lou, 84, 88, *89*, 92, 93, 99, 101, 105, 107, 109, 110, 114, 115, 118, 121, 123, 126, 127, *128*, 129, 136
Gehringer, Charlie, 96, 111, 118, 119
Gentile, Jim, 216
Giamatti, Bart, 327
Gibson, Bob, 229, 241, 242, 243, 245, 250
Gibson, Josh, 102
Gibson, Kirk, 309, 322, 324-325, *325*
Gibson, Sam, 89
Gilliam, Junior, 185
Gladden, Dan, 337
Glaviano, Tommy, 170
Glavine, Tom, 335, 353, 362
Gold Glove Award, 200, 204
Gomez, Lefty, 110, 120, 121
Gonzalez, Juan, 340, 342, 354, 363
Gooden, Dwight, 306, 310, 348
Goodman, Billy, 170
Gordon, Joe, 138, 211
Gordon, Tom, 365
Goslin, Goose, 80, 91
Gowdy, Hank, 51, 60
Graney, Jack, 51
Granger, Wayne, 248, 252
Grant, "Harvard" Eddie, 63
Gray, Pete, 150
Green, Dallas, 293
Green, Pumpsie, 207
Greenberg, Hank, 112, *113*, 114, 120, 122, 130, 131, 132, 153, 155, 158, 317
Gregg, Vean, 40
Grich, Bobby, 263, 312
Griffey, Ken, Jr., 328, 332, 348, *358*, *361*
Griffey, Ken, Sr., 328, 332

Griffith, Calvin, 192
Griffith, Clark, 110
Griffith Stadium (Washington), 171
Grimes, Burleigh, 41, 71, 111
Grimes, Ray, 73
Grimm, Charlie, 105
Groat, Dick, 211
Groh, Heinie, 80
Grove, Lefty, 85, 94, 97, 99, 100, *101*, 102, 106, 127, 137
Guidry, Ron, 282, 284
Gullickson, Bill, 293
Gutierrez, Cesar, 252
Gwynn, Tony, 307, 318, 323, 328, 348, 349, 353, 355, 359, 366

H
Haas, Mule, 103
Hack, Stan, 153
Haddix, Harvey, 207
Hadley, Bump, 119
Haefner, Milton, 157
Hafey, Chick, 101
Hahn, Noodles, 12
Hall of Fame, 116, 127, 132, 219
Hamilton, Jack, 239
Hammaker, Atlee, 305
Hansen, Ron, 244
Hargrave, Bubbles, 85, 122
Harris, Joe, 26
Hartnett, Gabby, 97, 112, 125
Hatcher, Billy, 333
Hauser, Joe, 81, 107
Hawkins, Andy, 331
Heath, Jeff, 137
Heilmann, Harry, 70, 73, 76, 82, 88, 98
Henderson, Dave, 317
Henderson, Rickey, 293, 296, 298, 299, 303, 311, 328, 330, 336, 337, 341
Hendrick, George, 301
Henrich, Tommy, 137
Hentgen, Pat, 354
Herman, Babe, 87, 114
Hernandez, Keith, 285, 286, 292

Hernandez, Livan, 361
Hernandez, Willie, 306
Hershberger, Willard, 131
Hershiser, Orel, 322, 324, 325
Herzog, Buck, 56
Higgins, Pinky, 124
Hiller, John, 263
Hirschbeck, John, 357
Hitchcock, Sterling, 365
Hobson, Butch, 284
Hodges, Gil, 171, 200, 239, 258
Hoffman, Trevor, 365
Holloman, Bobo, 184
Holmes, Tommy, 150
Holtzman, Kenny, 239
homer in the gloaming, 125
Hooper, Harry, 54
Horlen, Joe, 241
Horner, Bob, 316
Hornsby, Rogers, 58, 68, 70, 72, 74, 76, 79, 80, 82, 85, 86, 87, 90, 91, 93, 94, 225
Houston, Til, 49
Houston Astros, 255, 289, 293, 317, 369
Houston Colt .45s, 216, 225, 242, 248
Howard, Elston, 192, 222
Howard, Frank, 244, 253
Howe, Steve, 304
Howser, Dick, 291
Hoyt, LaMarr, 302
Hoyt, Waite, 72
Hrbek, Kent, 295
Hubbell, Carl, 106, 108, 109, 110, 115, 117, 118, 121
Hubbs, Ken, 229
Hudlin, Willis, 131
Huelsman, Frank, 21
Huggins, Miller, 95
Hughson, Tex, 139
Hundley, Randy, 244
Hunt, Ron, 255, 269
Hunter, Catfish, 245, 261, 268, 271
Huntington Grounds (Boston), 18
Hurst, Don, 105

I
Irabu, Hideki, 367
Irvin, Monte, 177

J
Jackson, Bo, 315
Jackson, Joe, 40, 44, 47, 53, 56, 65, 66, 66, 67, 328
Jackson, Reggie, 262, 272, 277, 281, 293, 300, 307, 320
Jacobs Field (Cleveland), 347
Jacobson, Baby Doll, 72
Janowicz, Vic, 183
Jansen, Larry, 174
Jarry Park (Montreal), 246
Jaster, Larry, 236
Jay, Joey, 216
Jenkins, Ferguson, 254, 268
Jensen, Jackie, 172, 202, 208
Jensen, Woody, 116
John, Tommy, 241
Johnson, Alex, 251
Johnson, Ban, 90
Johnson, Dave, 264
Johnson, Howard, 335
Johnson, Ken, 227
Johnson, Lance, 356
Johnson, Randy, 342, 351, 367
Johnson, Walter, 30, 31, 37, 44, 46, 50, 52, 55, 56, 61, 64, 67, 79, 81, 83, 84, 90, 116
Jones, Davy, 26
Jones, Randy, 274
Jones, Toothpick Sam, 191, 204
Jordan, Michael, 347
Joss, Addie, 32, 41

K
Kaat, Jim, 219, 233, 237
Kahn, Roger, 151
Kaline, Al, 190, 200, 238, 260, 269
Kamm, Willie, 74, 92
Kansas City Royals, 246, 279, 280-281, 291, 293, 313
Karl, Andy, 151
Kavanagh, Marty, 56
Keane, Johnny, 231

Keeler, Willie, 12
Keister, Bill, 18
Kekich, Mike, 263
Keller, Charlie, 129
Kelly, George, 78
Kennedy, Bill, 156
Kennedy, John, 201
Kerr, Dickie, 71
Kessinger, Don, 211
Killebrew, Harmon, 192, 208, 219, 222, 233, 246, 256
Killefer, Red, 56
Kiner, Ralph, 155, 159, 163, 167, 168, 174, 179
Kingdome (Seattle), 349
Kingman, Dave, 287, 300
Klein, Chuck, 94, 98, 100, 103, 106-107, 117
Klein, Lou, 145
Kluszewski, Ted, 187, 192
Knight, Ray, 317
Knoop, Bobby, 235
Konstanty, Jim, 170
Koosman, Jerry, 249
Koslo, Dave, 167
Koufax, Sandy, 207, 220, 222, 223, 225, 228-229, 230, 231, 233, 234, 236, 237
Kralick, Jack, 220
Krause, Harry, 35
Kroc, Ray, 268
Kuenn, Harvey, 182, 206, 211
Kuhel, Joe, 152
Kuhn, Bowie, 246, 265, 269, 274, 308
Kuiper, Duane, 280
Kull, John, 36

L
Labine, Clem, 197
Lajoie, Nap, 10, *11*, 12, 16, 17, 20, 23, 37, 38, 39, 50
Lamb, Lyman, 81
Landis, Kenesaw Mountain, 67, 90, 108, 144, 149
Lansford, Carney, 296
Larkin, Barry, 350
Larkin, Gene, 337

Larsen, Don, 196, *197*
Lary, Frank, 212
Lary, Lyn, 110
Lasorda, Tom, 276, 295
Laudner, Tim, 295
Lavagetto, Cookie, 161
Law, Vern, 210
Lazzeri, Tony, 83, 117
Leach, Tommy, 15
Lee, Bill, 122
LeFlore, Ron, 267, 276, 284
Lehner, Paul, 175
Lemon, Bob, 164, 171, 179, 187, 191, 283, 287
Lemon, Chet, 279
Lennon, Bob, 189
Leonard, Dutch, 50
Levsen, Dutch, 85
Levy, David, 119
Leyland, Jim, 360
Lindstrom, Freddy, 93
Litwhiler, Danny, 140
Lockman, Whitey, 176
Lofton, Kenny, 348
Lolich, Mickey, 244, 245, 254
Lollar, Sherm, 200
Lombardi, Ernie, 122, 133
Lonborg, Jim, 239
Long, Dale, 194
Lopat, Ed, 177, 185
Lopes, Davey, 271
Lopez, Al, 159
Los Angeles Angels, 214
Los Angeles Dodgers, 199, 202, 209, 220, 221, 225, 233, 237, 269, 279, 281, 283, 285, 297, 324
Louisville Red Birds, 303
Lucas, Red, 120, 124
Lush, John, 21
Lyle, Sparky, 279
Lynn, Fred, 270, 286, 304
Lyons, Ted, 139

M
Mack, Connie, 10, 24, 36, 38, 39, 171, 196
Mack, Earl, 38

MacPhail, Larry, 141, 161
Maddox, Garry, 293, 299
Maddux, Greg, 338, 343, 344, 347, 351
Madlock, Bill, 271, 276, 296, 303
Magee, Sherry, 37, 51
Maglie, Sal, 171, 174
Maloney, Jim, 231, 249
Malzone, Frank, 200
Mantle, Mickey, 176, 181, 184, 185, 191, 194, 198, 204, *205,* 212, 214, 217, 218, 225, 229, 238, 353
Manush, Heinie, 86, 91, 107
Marberry, Firpo, 80, 86
Marcum, Johnny, 114
Marichal, Juan, 211, 237, 244
Marion, Marty, 146
Maris, Roger, 210, 214, *215,* 217, 225
Marquard, Rube, 45
Marshall, Mike, 268
Martin, Billy, 185, 248, 272, 281, 283, 287, 291, 323, 328
Martin, Pepper, 102
Martinez, Dennis, 334
Martinez, Edgar, 339, 351
Martinez, Pedro, 359, 367
Mathews, Eddie, 182, 201, 206, 217, 240
Mathewson, Christy, 17, 18, 19, 21, 22, *23,* 24, 28, 31, 33, 35, 38, 41, 47, 56, 60, 62, 84, 116
Mathewson, Henry, 27
Mattingly, Don, 307, 310, 315, 320
Mays, Carl, 67, 71, 77
Mays, Willie, 176, 186, *188,* 189, 192, 194, 200, 204, *205,* 212, 214, 217, 218, 228, 230, 243, 252
Mazeroski, Bill, 211, 213, *213*
McCarthy, Joe, 102, 105, 129
McCarver, Tim, 229, 261
McCormick, Frank, 128, 130, 133
McCormick, Mike, 239
McCovey, Willie, 209, 221, 222, 244, 247
McDaniel, Lindy, 210
McDowell, Jack, 342
McDowell, Sam, 233
McGee, Willie, 310, 332
McGinnity, Joe, 17, 19, 20
McGraw, John, 13, 24, 26, 72, 81, 103, 108, 109
McGraw, Tug, 293
McGriff, Fred, 338
McGwire, Mark, 318, 354, *355,* 359, 362, 364, 366
McInnis, Stuffy, 71
McIntire, Harry, 27
McKechnie, Bill, 56, 93, 129, 309
McLain, Denny, 242, 243, 247, 253
McMillan, Roy, 200
McNally, Dave, 248, 257, 270
McNamara, John, 324
McQuinn, George, 124, 149
McRae, Hal, 274, 280, 299
McSherry, John, 356
Medich, Doc, 299
Medwick, Ducky, 116, 118, 125
Medwick, Joe, *120*
Melton, Bill, *255*
Merkle, Fred, 32
Mertes, Sam, 15
Mesa, Jose, 351
Messersmith, Andy, 270
Metrodome (Minnesota), 299, 321
Meusel, Bob, 75, 82
Mexican League, 155, 171
Miller, Marvin, 235
Miller, Stu, 204, 239
Milwaukee (AL), 13
Milwaukee Braves, 183, 185, 200, 201, 204, 205, 209, 216, 236
Milwaukee Brewers, 250, 301, 320, 363
Minnesota Twins, 210, 214, 224, 233, 237, 289, 321, 332, 336, 337

Minoso, Minnie, 200, 276
Mitchell, Kevin, 326
Mize, Johnny, 125, 127, 130, 159, 161, 163
Molitor, Paul, 301, 319, 335, 343, 356
Monbouquette, Bill, 220
Monday, Rick, 231, 297
Money, Don, 268
Montanez, Willie, 255
Montreal Expos, 246, 336
Moore, Earl, 11
Moore, Terry, 145
Moore, Wilcy, 88
Moose, Bob, 261
Morandini, Mickey, 341
Morgan, Joe, 270, 273, 274, 284, 309, 324
Morris, Jack, 309, 337
Mota, Manny, 290
Mueller, Les, 152
Mueller, Ray, 147
Mulcahy, Hugh, 134
Mullin, George, 30, 34
Munson, Thurman, 274, 287
Murderer's Row, 90
Murphy, Dale, 298, 302, 307, 313
Murphy, Johnny, 127
Murray, Eddie, 353, 356
Murtaugh, Danny, 212
Musial, Stan, 142, 148, 152, 154, 162, *165*, 167, 170, 174, 178, 187, 198, 202, 208, 224
Mussina, Mike, 360
Myer, Buddy, 113
Myers, Hy, 65
Myers, Randy, 333, 343

N
Nagy, Charles, 361
Navin Field (Detroit), 43
Negro Leagues, 68, 102, 163, 212
Nehf, Art, 61
Nettles, Graig, 255, 283, 285
Neun, Johnny, 90

Newcombe, Don, 191, 194
Newhouser, Hal, 146, *148*, 150, 153, 154
New York (AL), 16
New York Giants, 21, 24, 42, 45, 48, 55, 56, 60, 62, 65, 72, 78, 81, 96, 108, 117, 121, 124, 160, 176, 189, 199
New York Highlanders, 21, 32, 46
New York Mets, 216, 218, 223, 226, 230, 239, 242, 249, 257, 264-265, 280, 317, 324, 357, 369
New York Yankees, 46, 49, 53, 61, 67, 72, 75, 77, 78, 87, 89, 90, 93, 96, 99, 102, 105, 110, 112, 117, 121, 124, 125, 129, 132, 137, 140, 141, 144, 145, 156, 159, 161, 169, 173, 177, 181, 185, 188, 189, 193, 195, 196, 201, 205, 212, 213, 217, 221, 225, 229, 231, 234, 243, 269, 277, 281, 285, 297, 300, 353, 357, 362, 365, 369
Nichols, Chet, 176
Nicholson, Bill, 142, 147
Nicholson, Dave, 224
Niekro, Joe, 287
Niekro, Phil, 287, 312, 319
Nieman, Bob, 175
Nomo, Hideo, 353
Nuxhall, Joe, 147

O
Oakland Athletics, 242, 260, 261, 265, 269, 271, 291, 297, 324, 328, 329, 333, 356
O'Brien, Eddie, 185
O'Brien, Johnny, 185
O'Connell, Jimmy, 81
O'Connor, Jack, 38, 39
Odom, Blue Moon, 260
O'Doul, Lefty, 95, 104
Oeschger, Joe, 68

O'Farrell, Bob, 85
Oglivie, Ben, 293
Oh, Sadaharu, 266
Ojeda, Bob, 343
Olerud, John, 343
Olin, Steve, 343
Oliva, Tony, 226, 230, 232, 236, 237, 255
Oliver, Al, 300
Olivo, Diomedes, 220
Olson, Gregg, 327
Olympic Stadium (Montreal), 278, 336
O'Malley, Walter, 180
$100,000 infield, 47
O'Neill, Jack, 15
O'Neill, Mike, 15
O'Neill, Paul, 348
Oriole Park at Camden Yards (Baltimore), 340
Orta, Jorge, 313
Orth, Al, 26
Ott, Mel, 86, 95, 104, 111, 120, 121, 125, 139, 143
Owen, Mickey, 137

P
Padgett, Ernie, 77
Page, Joe, 167
Paige, Satchel, 163, 180, 231
Palmer, Jim, 262, 270, 274
Pappas, Milt, 259
Park, Chan Ho, 368
Parker, Dave, 280, 283, 313
Parnell, Mel, 166
Parrott, Mike, 291
Passeau, Claude, 153
Peckinpaugh, Roger, 49, 82, 84
Pendleton, Terry, 334
Perez, Tony, 239
Perry, Gaylord, 250, 259, 282, 299
Perry, Jim, 250
Pesky, Johnny, 139, 155, 157
Peters, Gary, 241
Peterson, Fritz, 263
Pettitte, Andy, 354
Pfiester, Jack, 28

Philadelphia Athletics, 10, 12, 15, 23, 24, 36, 39, 42, 48, 51, 54, 89, 96, 99, 102, 103, 114, 126, 132, 144, 152, 164, 167
Philadelphia Phillies, 35, 54, 65, 73, 93, 96, 107, 123, 132, 136, 138, 173, 201, 216, 229, 276, 287, 293, 305, 344
Philley, Dave, 208, 216
Phillippe, Deacon, 12, 18
Piazza, Mike, 344, 351, 360
Pipp, Wally, 59
Pittsburgh Pirates, 12, 15, 17, 18, 30, 35-36, 68, 84, 156, 172, 180, 204, 212-213, 257, 269, 271, 289, 341
Plank, Eddie, 24, 52, 224
Podres, Johnny, 193, 196
Pollet, Howie, 145, 157
Polo Grounds (New York), 32, 41, 78, 176, 189, 225
Porter, Darrell, 289
Powell, Boog, 237, 250
Powers, Jimmy, 160
Pride, Curtis, 344
Prim, Ray, 153
Puckett, Kirby, 321, 324, 326, 339, 348
Puhl, Terry, 328
Pulliam, Harry, 14, 21, 35

Q
Quinn, Jack, 99
Quisenberry, Dan, 303

R
Radatz, Dick, 224, 226
Raines, Tim, 296, 304, 319
Ramirez, Manny, 366
Raschi, Vic, 171, 172
Reardon, Jeff, 340
Redland Field (Cincinnati), 43
Reese, Pee Wee, 161
Reiser, Pete, 135, 157, 161
Renteria, Edgar, 361
Repulski, Rip, 187

Reulbach, Ed, 32
Reynolds, Allie, 181
Rhodes, Dusty, 189
Rice, Jim, 270, 279, 282, 303
Rice, Sam, 81, 83, 99
Richard, J.R., 255, 289, 290
Richards, Paul, 211
Richardson, Bill, 221
Richardson, Bobby, 217, 229
Richert, Pete, 256
Rickey, Branch, 29, 56, 141, 151, 180, 210
Riddle, Elmer, 136
Righetti, Dave, 316
Rijo, Jose, 333
Ring, Jimmy, 87
Ripken, Billy, 320
Ripken, Cal, Jr., 302, 312, 320, 334, 352, *352*, 363
Ripken, Cal, Sr., 320
Ripple, Jimmy, 133
Rivera, Mariano, 369
Riverfront Stadium (Cincinnati), 252
Rixey, Eppa, 75
Rizzuto, Phil, 141, 170, 171, 173
Roberts, Robin, 178, 184, 190
Roberts, Thomas, 319
Robertson, Charlie, 75
Robertson, Dave, 59
Robinson, Brooks, 226, *228*, 237, 253, 280
Robinson, Frank, 195, 215, 220, 234, *235*, 237, 256, 271
Robinson, Jackie, 151, 155, 159, *159*, 160, 161, 166, 181, 197, 219, 260
Rodriguez, Alex, 355, 363
Roe, Preacher, 175
Rogers, Kenny, 347
Rogers, Steve, 297
Rolen, Scott, 358
Rolfe, Red, 127
Rommel, Eddie, 73, 105
Root, Charlie, 88
Rosar, Buddy, 155
Rose, Pete, 224, 247, 262, 268, 272, 276, 283, 287, 294, 304, 305, 307, 311, *311*, 315, 327
Rosen, Al, 172, 181, 182, 188
Roush, Edd, 56, 58, 64, 65
Rowe, Schoolboy, 111
Rudi, Joe, 274
Ruffing, Red, 124, 141
Runnels, Pete, 219
Ruppert, Jake, 49
Ruth, Babe, 50, 51, 53, 54, 55, 56, 57, 59, 61, 62, 63, 64, 67, *69*, 70, 72, 73, 75, 76, 78, 79, 82, 86, 87, 88, *89*, 90, 92, 93, 94, 98, 101, 103, *104*, 105, 106, 107, 110, 111, 112, 113, 116, 163
Ryan, Jack, 34
Ryan, Nolan, 257, 260, 264, 271, 276, 279, 289, 295, 302, 312, 320, 327, 331, 336, 344
Rye, Gene, 99

S

Saberhagen, Bret, 310, 313, 326, 348
Sabo, Chris, 333
Sain, Johnny, 163, 164
Sandberg, Ryne, 306, *308*, 332, 347
Sanders, Deion, 341
San Diego Padres, 246, 268, 309, 357, 365, 367
Sanford, Jack, 219, 221
San Francisco Giants, 199, 202, 209, 220, 221, 226, 257, 321, 329, 358, 365
Santiago, Benito, 319
Sauer, Hank, 178
Schaefer, Herman, 26
Scheib, Carl, 144
Schilling, Curt, 359
Schmidt, Mike, 266, 272, 275, 290, 293, 295, 300, 304, 308, 314
Schneider, Pete, 78
Schoendienst, Red, 170
Schott, Marge, 344

Schulte, Wildfire, 40
Score, Herb, 190, 195, 199
Scott, Everett, 78, 84, 107
Scott, George, 272
Scott, Jim, 51
Scott, Mike, 314
Seaton, Tom, 47
Seattle Mariners, 278, 304, 316, 349, 353, 356, 359
Seattle Pilots, 246, 250
Seaver, Tom, 238, 246, 247, 251, 256, 262, 263, 270, 280, 312, 315
Seerey, Pat, 163
Seitz, Peter, 270
Selig, Bud, 340, 363
Sentell, Paul, 26
Sewell, Joe, 83, 95
Seymour, Cy, 22
Shantz, Bobby, 178, 200
Shea, Spec, 161
Shea Stadium (New York), 227
Sheffield, Gary, 338
Shepard, Bert, 151
Sherry, Larry, 209
Shibe Park (Philadelphia), 34, 73, 123, 126, 144, 179
Shore, Ernie, 59
shot heard 'round the world, 176
Shotton, Burt, 161, 169
Sianis, Billy, 153
Sierra, Ruben, 326
Siever, Ed, 15
Sievers, Roy, 200
Simmons, Al, 84, 96, 97, 99, 103, 110
Simmons, Ted, 272
Sisler, Dick, 173
Sisler, George, 68, 72, 73, 74, 83
Skowron, Bill, 205, 217
SkyDome (Toronto), 328
Slaughter, Enos, 141, 145, 156, 157
Smith, Bob, 90
Smith, Lee, 335, 340
Smith, Lonnie, 301, 335
Smith, Ozzie, 291, 313, 328, 340
Smith, Red, 107

Smith, Reggie, 279
Smith, Sherry, 57
Smoltz, John, 336-337, 355
Snider, Duke, 169, 172, 181, 192, 195, 199
Snodgrass, Fred, 45
Sosa, Sammy, 362, 366
Spahn, Warren, 160, 164, 168, 175, 185, 198, 203, 204, 212, 216, 224, 232
Spalding, Al, 30
Speaker, Tris, 35, 43, 50, 55, 68, 76, 83, 90, 92
Spooner, Karl, 255
St. Louis Browns, 13, 56, 87, 129, 143, 148, 149, 172, 175, 186
St. Louis Cardinals, 56, 87, 93, 99, 102, 111, 124, 141, 145, 147, 149, 157, 168, 169, 172, 175, 229, 241, 245, 269, 300, 301, 313, 321
Stahl, Chick, 27, 28
Stallard, Tracy, 214
Stanky, Eddie, 151
Stanley, Bob, 300
Stargell, Willie, 254, 263, 286, 288, 289
Staub, Rusty, 265, 305
Steinbrenner, George, 263, 269, 283, 333
Stengel, Casey, 46, 144, 165, 168-169, 173, 177, 185, 213, 227, 272
Stennett, Rennie, 271
Stephens, Gene, 184
Stephens, Vern, 167
Sterling, Leslie, 349
Stewart, Dave, 329, 345
Stieb, Dave, 323
Stirnweiss, Snuffy, 147, 151
Stockton, J. Roy, 110
Stone, George, 25
Stone, Steve, 290
Strand, Paul, 78
Strawberry, Darryl, 323
Subway Series, 72, 75, 121
Suhr, Gus, 118

Sullivan, Frank, 191
Surkont, Max, 184
Sutcliffe, Rick, 306
Sutter, Bruce, 286, 291, 307
Sutton, Don, 312, 316
Suzuki, Mac, 367
Sweeney, Bill, 49
Swift, Bill, 340

T

Tabor, Jim, 127
Taft, William, 37
"Take Me Out to the Ballgame," 33
Tampa Bay Devil Rays, 362
Tatis, Fernando, 368
Taylor, Jack, 20, 26
Tekulve, Kent, 285, 289
Templeton, Gary, 288
Tenace, Gene, 261
Tener, John K., 62
Terry, Bill, 97, 101, 103, 108, 221
Texas Rangers, 258, 303, 358, 369
Thigpen, Bobby, 332
Thomas, Bill, 180
Thomas, Frank, 342, 346, 356, 359
Thomas, Gorman, 287, 300
Thompson, Homer, 45
Thompson, Tommy, 45
Thomson, Bobby, 176, 177
Thon, Dickie, 309
Three Rivers Stadium (Pittsburgh), 252
Tiant, Luis, 242
Tiger Stadium (Detroit), 43
Tinker, Joe, 15, 33, 39, 49
Tobin, Jack, 72
Tobin, Jim, 140, 147
Toney, Fred, 59
Toporcer, Specs, 71
Topps baseball cards, 176
Toronto Blue Jays, 278, 287, 313, 320, 328, 336, 337, 341, 345
Torre, Joe, 254, 357, 369

Torrez, Mike, 281
Tovar, Cesar, 244
Trammell, Alan, 309, 353
Trebelhorn, Tom, 347
Trosky, Hal, 110, 115
Trout, Dizzy, 146
Trucks, Virgil, 179
Turley, Bob, 202
Turner, Jim, 119
Turner, Ted, 276

U

Ueberroth, Peter, 308
Uhle, George, 71, 85
umpires, 367
Underwood, Pat, 288
Underwood, Tom, 288
Unser, Del, 293

V

Valentin, John, 347
Valenzuela, Fernando, 294, 295
Vance, Dazzy, 79, 83, 91, 97
Vander Meer, Johnny, 123
Vaughan, Arky, 112
Vaughn, Hippo, 59, 62
Vaughn, Mo, 350, 351
Veeck, Bill, 163, 175, 208, 210, 296
Ventura, Robin, 367
Vernon, Mickey, 155, 183
Versalles, Zoilo, 230
Veterans Stadium (Philadelphia), 255
Vincent, Fay, 329, 333, 340
Viola, Frank, 321, 322
Virdon, Bill, 272
Vitt, Ossie, 130
Voiselle, Bill, 149
Vosmik, Joe, 113
Vuckovich, Pete, 298

W

Waddell, Rube, 17, 19, 22, 24, 29, 51
Wagner, Honus, 10, 13, 20, 25, 28, 29, 31, 34, 41, 48, 50, 116

Wakefield, Dick, 136, 144
Walker, Bill, 96, 101
Walker, Dixie, 146, 151, 161
Walker, Harry, 157, 158
Walker, Larry, 358, 366
Walsh, Ed, 11, 28, 31
Walters, Bucky, 126, 131, 133
Wambsganss, Bill, 69
Waner, Lloyd, 89
Waner, Paul, 89, 104, 110, 115, 139
Warhop, Jack, 53
Warneke, Lon, 104
Washington Senators, 12, 21, 29, 41, 48, 81, 84, 108, 151, 152, 192, 199, 210, 258
Wathan, John, 300
Watkins, George, 99
Watson, Bob, 271
Weaver, Earl, 253, 305
Webb, Earl, 102
Weeghman, Charlie, 56
Weeghman Field (Chicago), 50
Weiss, Walt, 322
Welch, Bob, 330
Wells, David, 363
Wertz, Vic, 189
Wetteland, John, 356
Wheat, Zach, 62
Whitaker, Lou, 353
White, Doc, 26
Whiten, Mark, 344, 365
Wilhelm, Hoyt, 179, 203, 211, 248
Wilhoit, Joe, 65
Williams, Billy, 252, 258
Williams, Cy, 76
Williams, Dick, 265, 309
Williams, Earl, 255
Williams, Ken, 74, 75
Williams, Lefty, 66, 67
Williams, Matt, 348
Williams, Mitch, 345
Williams, Ted, 127, 134, 138, *140*, 141, 154, 157, 158, 163, 166, 173, 178, 186, 198, 200, 203, 208, 211, 248

Willis, Vic, 20, 23
Wills, Maury, 218, 220, 225
Wilson, Chief, 45
Wilson, Don, 249
Wilson, Earl, 220
Wilson, Hack, 86, 91, 94, 97, *98*
Wilson, Jimmie, 133
Wilson, Mookie, 317
Wilson, Willie, 291, 300
Winfield, Dave, 287, 341
Wise, Rick, 256
Witt, Mike, 307
Wohlers, Mark, 353
Wood, Jake, 217
Wood, Joe, 43, *44*
Wood, Kerry, 363
Wood, Wilbur, 263
Worrell, Todd, 315
Wright, Glenn, 84
Wright, Taffy, 136
Wrigley, William, 70, 215
Wrigley Field (Chicago), 50, 78, 153, 322
Wyatt, Johnny, 227
Wynn, Early, 171, 175, 179, 187, 206, 225
Wyse, Hank, 153

Y

Yankee Stadium (New York), 77
Yastrzemski, Carl, 222, 232, 238, *240*, 243, 251, 288, 299
Yawkey, Tom, 108
York, Rudy, 119, 131, 132, 142
Yost, Eddie, 208
Young, Anthony, 344
Young, Cy, 10, 14, *14*, 20, 22, 29, 34, 37, 41
Youngblood, Joel, 299
Yount, Robin, 298, 326, 340

Z

Zernial, Gus, 175
Zimmerman, Heinie, 43, 60